BBC Books, an imprint of Ebury Publishing
20 Vauxhall Bridge Road, London SW1V 2SA

BBC Books is part of the Penguin Random House group of companies
whose addresses can be found at global.penguinrandomhouse.com

Penguin
Random House
UK

This book is published to accompany the television series
Strictly Come Dancing first broadcast on BBC One in 2020.

Executive Producer: Sarah James
Series Director: Nikki Parsons
Series Producer: Lee English
Series Producer: Jack Gledhill
Series Editor: Robin Lee-Perrella

With thanks to: Harriet Frost, Selena Harvey, Claire Hore, Eve Winstanley, and
The BBC Pictures Team including: Catherine Yang, Anna Lenihan and Jane Record.

Pages 114/115: Do not follow these routines without first consulting a healthcare professional.

First published by BBC Books in 2020

www.penguin.co.uk

A CIP catalogue record for this book is available from the British Library.

ISBN 9781785945557

Printed and bound in Italy by L.E.G.O. S.p.A

Picture credits: Ray Burmiston/BBC © 4–6, 10, 12, 22, 24, 26, 32, 34, 42, 44, 46, 50, 52, 54,
60, 62, 64, 66, 68, 70, 74, 76, 78, 80, 82, 88, 90, 94, 96, 102, 104, 118, 120, 122, 124,
Guy Levy/BBC © 8, 28, 30, 48, 56, 58, 59, 84, 87, 98, 101, 106, 109, 112–3, Baby Steps 14–21
by respective pro dancers, Drawings 37–41 by respective pro dancers, Laretta Houston/ABC
© 72, Ian Waite © 110, Gethin Jones © 92

Strictly Come Dancing

ANNUAL 2021

BBC
BOOKS

CONTENTS

MEET THE PRO DANCERS

STRICTLY FEATURES

FUN AND TRIVIA

Motsi Mabuse

Making her debut on the judging panel last year, Motsi Mabuse impressed viewers with her bubbly personality and encouraging critiques. Now the South African-born dancer, who has also been a judge on the German version of the show for nine years, is excited to be returning to *Strictly* for the new series.

'My first year on the show was amazing,' she says. 'From the beginning until the end, I was still thinking, "I can't believe I'm part of this." So, after a little bit of time away, I'm looking forward to being in the show without feeling I have to pinch myself.'

Motsi, who started competing in national championships in South Africa as a teenager, says she and her fellow judges all bring something different to the table.

'I feel I'm bringing a different type of vibe and energy,' she says. 'I come from the dance world and, of course, I know all the basics, the technique, etc., but that is not all I look for in a dance. I'm all about the feeling, the energy, and about pushing people onwards. I see myself as a motivational judge.'

Her fellow judges, she says, welcomed her with open arms and helped her settle into her new role.

'Shirley, Bruno and Craig were brilliant,' she says. 'Everybody was professional to the highest level, which is very important to me. But they were also welcoming and friendly – and a lot of fun.'

Motsi, who lives in Germany, is impressed with this year's line-up and is looking forward to seeing the new contestants strut their stuff.

'I saw Maisie Smith dance last year on Children in Need and she was great,' she says. 'I have seen HRVY do some moves and I thought that he did well, and Max George too. It's good to see Jamie Laing getting a second chance. I think he's going to bring a fun side to the show.

'I'm glad that we've made that step of inclusiveness and included a different type of couple than we are used to, having Nicola Adams dancing with a female pro,' she says. '*Strictly* is so diverse and we should open our diversity to everybody and lead by example.'

After an amazing year last year, Motsi believes this series is set to be every bit as spectacular. 'People are looking for a good time and I'm looking forward to being back in the studio and bringing all the excitement and the magical atmosphere of *Strictly* to the audience at home.'

Former *Emmerdale* star Kelvin Fletcher, who lifted the series 16 trophy with Oti Mabuse, says his family and friends were used to seeing him strut his stuff on the dance floor before *Strictly*, but never in a choreographed routine.

I'm always first on the dance floor at weddings,' he says. 'It's usually the women who get up first, but I'll be up there with my nan and my aunties, dancing away.

'But I've never followed choreography, so my family were shocked watching my Samba on the first night.'

One *Strictly* fan who was glued to the screen that night was Kelvin's mum, who sent him a touching message the following morning.

'I've been acting since I was six, I've won awards and played at the Palladium, but the text she sent me that morning will stay with me forever,' he recalls.

'She listed all the things I'd achieved, saying,

"You won Oldham's Beautiful Baby when you were first born, you won a soap award," and so on, even including random things like Easter Bunny competitions and a school sports race, which I'd completely forgotten.

'Then she said, "But I've never been as proud as I was last night." I was in tears. She's always been my biggest supporter, but to read something like that, the morning after an amazing night, meant so much.'

Kelvin certainly got off to a flying start, scoring an impressive 32 for his week-1 Samba – and he even surprised himself.

'I'd never done a Cha-cha-cha or a Waltz and I wasn't even trained as an actor. So to jump in and go through intense dance training meant I was out of my comfort zone, but that was part of the challenge that I was looking forward to.

'Within the first couple of days, I realised how physically demanding it was and that to stay in the competition, from week to week, is a real feat, so I vowed to work as hard as I possibly could and be the best version of myself.'

Starting from scratch every Monday meant every week was a journey for Kelvin.

'On Monday I was shown a routine, by Wednesday I still wasn't getting it, but somehow by Thursday or Friday it clicked,' he says.

'Oti and I both have a strong work ethic. She set the bar high, but her belief in me was so high that it gave me a renewed sense of belief in myself.'

Despite getting strong scores every week, Kelvin's harshest critic was himself.

'Throughout the whole competition, the Quickstep was the only dance where I didn't make a single mistake, by my own standards,' he says.'I'd have a really good week, but once the excitement and adrenaline came together on a Saturday, I was dancing on emotion and there were tiny mistakes that perhaps only I noticed.

'But Oti told me, "Don't worry. Just keep dancing and enjoy it." That's why I was able to perform through my mistakes and show that I was absolutely loving it.'

Kelvin, who has two children with wife Liz, says Movie Week and Musicals Week had a special meaning for him.

'The first time I took my three-year-old daughter Marnie to the cinema was to watch *Mary Poppins Returns*,' he explains.

'I'm a big believer that things are meant to be and when the Charleston came up in Movie Week, the song we were dancing to was "Trip a Little Light Fantastic".

'Further down the line, when I did my American Smooth, we'd just had four months of intense watching of *Beauty and the Beast*, and she was obsessed with Gaston.

'There I was, dancing to the Gaston song, and Luke Evans, who played Gaston in the film, was there so I got to meet him. It was amazing.'

Actor-turned-racing-driver Kelvin is used to speed, but even he was surprised at how quickly he found himself on the dance floor when he was asked to step in for the injured Jamie Laing.

'I wasn't on standby, so it came out of the blue,' he explains.

'I got a call asking if I wanted to do it and the following morning I was having a medical and starting rehearsals.

'I wasn't expecting it, but I've always wanted to do *Strictly* because it's such a great show.'

Kelvin impressed the judges and viewers alike, dancing into the Final with Karim Zeroual and Emma Barton.

As he lifted the iconic glitterball, he was overcome with emotion.

'The main feeling was an overwhelming sense of gratitude towards everyone who had given me this opportunity,' he says.

'From the family supporting me and the *Strictly* fans I bumped into who told me they loved my dancing, to the amazing producers, camera crews, costume team, make-up team, the other celebrities, the other professionals and even the judges, whose critique was great every week.

'The Final was one of the most special nights I'll ever have and I wish I could relive it.

'I occasionally watch a few moments on the computer and it brings the biggest smile to my face, from ear to ear. To date, winning *Strictly* is my proudest career achievement.'

Kelvin Fletcher

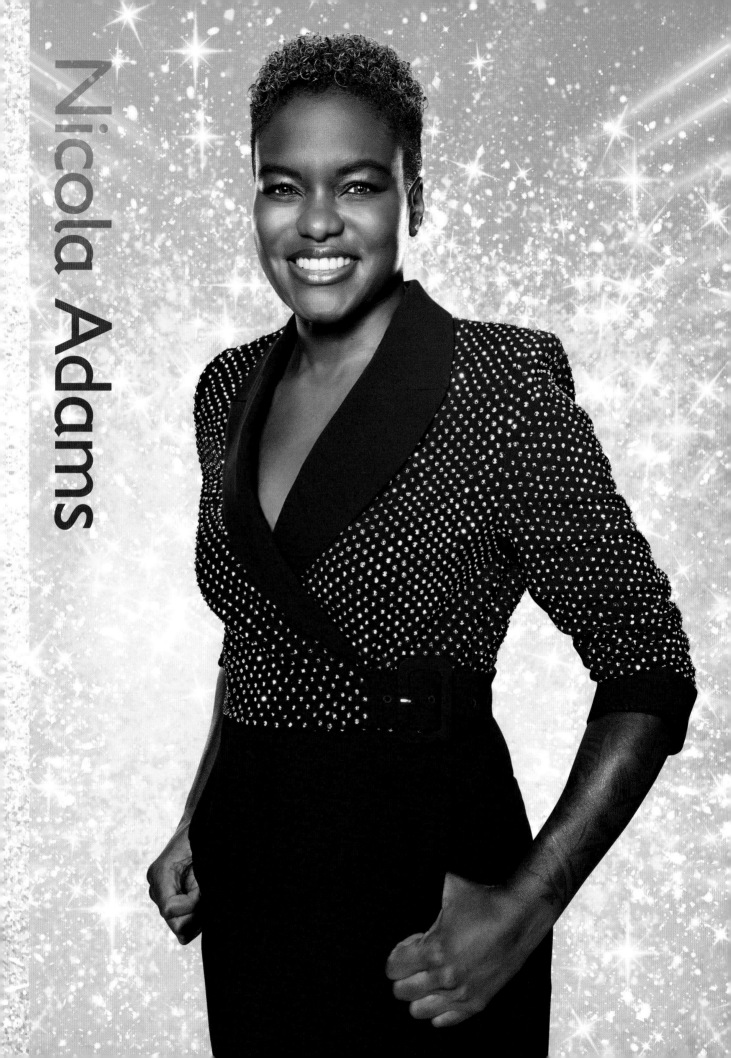

Nicola Adams

Nicola Adams is swapping the boxing ring for the dance floor but feels the agility she has as a World Champion boxer will be an asset on the show.

'I'll have the fitness side down,' she says. 'I'm quite light on my feet and in the ring I need to be on my toes. A lot of the dances you have to be on your toes, so I'm hoping that gives me an advantage.

'Also, the live performance side is a lot easier for me because I'm used to performing in front of big crowds of 20,000 people. But this is going to be a huge challenge, just because it's totally out of my comfort zone. I am used to the boxing ring and this is a totally different kind of arena, a different kind of learning routine. But it is going to be exciting and I'm looking forward to it.'

The Olympic gold medallist will be the first celebrity to dance in a same-sex partnership on the show, after requesting a female partner.

'It means a lot to me. I think it's a brilliant step in the right direction. And women actually dance with women all the time, both in nightclubs and on the professional circuit, so I guess it's just showing people that it can be done.'

The Leeds-born flyweight took on her first bout at 13 and, in 2001, became the first woman boxer to represent England. As an amateur she won every set of World, Commonwealth and European championships available to her, including two Olympic golds, at London 2012 and Rio 2016. She boxed professionally for two years, retiring in 2019.

Having been an athlete from an early age means Nicola is ready for any constructive criticism the judges can throw at her.

'I'm used to having really tough coaches,' she says. 'I think it's important to be able to take criticism, because that's how you progress and move forward. If I listen, the next time I go into the competition, I'll have worked on all those things that I did wrong and hopefully improve for the next performance.'

Used to long hours of training, Nicola says she will give the routines all she has, and expects the same from her partner.

'Whoever I'm partnered with, they have to be as competitive as me, because I'm going to be working hard every day and putting in as many hours as I possibly can,' she says. 'I'm definitely going to get frustrated at myself when I don't get the steps and the routine right. I'm super competitive and I want to be in the Final, so I'll be working as hard as I can to make that happen. If not, I'll have given 110 per cent, so I don't mind if I fall short.'

Since announcing her participation in the series, Nicola has been stunned at the reaction from fans and friends alike. 'It's been amazing,' she says. 'I've had lots of positive messages, everybody saying they can't wait to see me on Strictly, so I'm excited.

'The first person I told was my partner, Ella, and she's excited for me. My nan is over the moon because she's a big fan of the show, and my mum and all my friends are excited. They've all said, "You can't dance," but I can learn. I'm going out there to prove them wrong.'

Clara Amfo

Radio 1 star Clara Amfo is thrilled to be putting on her dancing shoes for *Strictly* and says she can't wait to embrace the whole experience.

'I always maintain that to have joy in your life is a human right and we need it,' she says. 'You're not put on this earth to suffer! *Strictly* is just unadulterated joy that everyone loves. It's an absolute fantasy world. I just want to be able to surrender myself to it, pretend to be a dancer and hopefully learn to be one in the process.'

As a DJ, Clara certainly has an ear for music, and she is hoping her feet can follow suit – especially when it comes to the elegant ballroom dances.

'I think it's Latin over ballroom for me,' she says. 'Ballroom scares me, because I only accepted a year or two ago that I'm quite a clumsy person. There isn't a week where I don't bang my elbow on the door or step on a plug. For me, to be graceful takes a lot of concentration.'

Clara says she will work hard to get the results she wants and is hoping her professional partner won't treat her with kid gloves.

'I'm very much a chemistry person,' she says. 'My gut always knows if I'm going to get on with someone, but I do need a partner who I'm going to vibe with as a friend. First and foremost, I think the basis of any good partnership is a decent friendship. But I also want someone who is going to push me. If I'm doing a step wrong, let's keep going until I get it right! I want fun to be the pinnacle of what we do, but I'm not afraid of hard work.'

Born in Kingston upon Thames, Clara started her career as an intern at Kiss FM before becoming a presenter, winning a Sony Radio Award in the Rising Star category in 2012. She moved on to shows on Radio 1Xtra, MTV and Radio 1, where she took over the mid-morning slot from Fearne Cotton in 2015. She also recently hosted *One World: Together at Home* for the BBC. Now she's hoping to add *Strictly* champ to her impressive list of achievements.

'To win would be an absolute dream, but at the same time, one piece of advice I was given was "you want to take it seriously, but you can't take it *too* seriously". It's just such a privilege to be in the show, a once-in-a-lifetime thing. No matter what happens, I can proudly say, "I was in *Strictly Come Dancing*," and there's only a finite number of people who can say that. I'm just genuinely happy to be here. Of course, I would love to last as long as I can. But at the same time, the great thing about the show is that you honestly don't know how it's going to turn out. Anything can happen! So I'm in it to win it, but with an asterisk.'

BABY STEPS

Everybody has to start somewhere, and for *Strictly*'s professional dancers training began at an early age. Here, the pros remember their first steps in a dance class – and why they fell in love with dancing as mere tots.

Giovanni Pernice

I started dancing when I was seven years old after seeing the TV show *Come Dancing*. I thought, 'This is how I want to spend the rest of my life.'

My first class was fun because my dance partner was my cousin, so we just went to have a bit of fun. I remember I did the Cha-cha-cha, and the teacher said, 'I think he's got charisma.' I was like, 'I know, darling!' Nothing's changed!

After my first class, I knew I wanted to carry on for the rest of my life, although, at seven, I didn't imagine it would be my job. But I received so many

compliments, because it's very hard to get boys dancing at that age, and I was the only one in the school. I liked the attention.

My mum and dad were very supportive, driving me to competitions outside of Sicily and also supporting me financially, because dancing is expensive. I was the first one in the family to dance, but then Mum and Dad started teaching and my sister followed in my footsteps and has her own studio in Sicily.

◀ Luba Mushtuk

I started dancing as soon as I could walk. That may sound impossible, but ballroom dancing is a very popular activity in Russia and they teach it at school. My big brother was already competing when I was born, and I was brought along to every dance class and competition he had. It was part of my life from the very start.

I was a bit of a naughty child and dancing focused me. All I needed was some music and the beautiful tulle skirt that my grandma made me, and I would be distracted, happily dancing in my own world.

My brother would teach me for fun and by the age of four I was already competing. My first partner was a little older, aged seven, and he was very embarrassed by me being so little, but we agreed we were never going to mention our age gap to anyone. Ever! The main joy for me was always the dresses. I still remember my first dress and my mum still has my very first pair of shoes at home. We might even frame them one day. Dancing was my biggest love from day one – and it will be forever.

Katya Jones ▶

Growing up in Russia, I took up ballroom dancing at six, and I started participating in school plays, along with singing, gymnastics, piano, languages, crafts and painting classes.

I was very shy and suffered from stage fright, which didn't go away for a long time, even when I started competing in ballroom dancing. My dad used to say I looked like a little duckling when I danced, because I never smiled. I was so tense my lips locked in a tight pout!

My mum was always very supportive, although we had many tears about my hair being plaited too tight or my make-up being wrong! I was the only dancer in the family and never knew who I got that talent from until recently, when my 57-year-old mother started dancing herself. It doesn't just bring tears to my eyes to see how naturally talented she is, it makes me feel like I am still the little duckling, because she is definitely the beautiful dancing swan of the family.

◀ Karen Hauer

Funnily enough, my first memory of learning to dance was not knowing what to wear – so I turned up at my first class in jeans! I was almost nine and I remember that my favourite thing was to do a cartwheel and go into a split.

As a kid growing up in the Bronx, in New York, I was very focused and disciplined and I loved learning. It wasn't because somebody was telling me to; I really wanted to do well because I didn't want the teacher to feel bad or that she wasn't teaching the right thing.

My first class was African dance and I loved that they played live drums. The teacher used her body in such a beautiful way, rotating her arms and creating such lovely, cool shapes, which, as a kid, I found amazing. I thought she was incredible, and I fell in love with dance in those lessons.

Gorka Márquez ▶

When I was 11, growing up in Spain, my dad used to go to ballroom lessons because he wanted to surprise my mum. I would go with him in the afternoon, on a secret little adventure to the studio. I sat on the sidelines watching, until I started to learn all the steps and could do them myself. Suddenly I was dancing, and the family were asking, 'How did you learn that?'

After that I was enrolled in a class for ballroom and Latin – and the rest is history.

◄ Neil Jones

I grew up on an army complex in Hampshire, and when I was three my mum used to take my sister to ballet class at the studio across the road. One day I followed them on my bike to watch through the window, then I walked in and told my mum, 'I really want to do this.' So I started with ballet and I was the only boy in the class.

When I was about seven I'd moved on from ballet to judo and football, but it takes so long to get a new belt in judo, and I'd only had one football tournament and one silver medal in a year. Meanwhile my sister had joined a new dance school in our area and came home with a trophy or medal every week. So I thought, 'I want to start dancing. I want more trophies.' I signed up for Latin and ballroom classes at the new dance school and never looked back.

Dianne Buswell ►

I started dancing at four. I was introduced to the glitz and glamour of ballroom by my oldest brother Andrew, who had been dancing for a few years. During his lessons, I was the little girl in the pram watching the girls and boys twirl around on the dance floor, and I told my mum, 'That's what I want to do.'

Mum booked me into the kids' class on Saturday mornings and I was the youngest, but my brother held my hand through the lesson. I wasn't a shy girl, so I quickly told him to go away because I wanted to twirl on my own! I loved every second of it.

At the age of eight, the one boy that danced in my home town was looking for a dance partner to compete with and I was one of the girls he was trialling. I was so excited, I remember stealing some of Mum's perfume and lipstick and watching dancing videos to get extra tips and tricks. It must have worked because we competed together for over six years and ended up as one of the top juvenile couples in Australia.

I feel so lucky that I had the opportunities to dance so much as a little girl, and to have my brother sharing my passion, always by my side, was extra special. As a little girl my dream was to compete in Blackpool, but it was just too far and too costly. Twenty years later, the dream came true when I danced in Blackpool on *Strictly*. Dream. Believe. Achieve.

Dianne and her brother Andrew

◀ Aljaž Škorjanec

Ever since I can remember, my life has been connected to dance. My first memory of winning was on 13 March 1999, when I was nine and my dance partner, Valerija, and I won our very first national championship in Slovenia. It is the only trophy I take with me everywhere. The joy and the feeling of accomplishment was amazing, but not just for me.

My dad would drive me to countless dance studios, competitions and shows, waiting for hours and cheering me on, always with a cheerful and positive approach to everything. Whenever I needed a shoulder to lean on, or a voice of reason and compassion, my mum would have the answer, calming me down after a bad result and keeping me going. My little sister Lara's love for dance competed with mine and she never missed a competition – with the world's biggest smile and personality from day one. She once told off a reporter for not including younger categories on TV ... she was three! My best friend from day one. All of my wins and losses, we lived through together. So when I think of dance, I think of my family.

Nadiya Bychkova ▶

When I was four, my grandmother took me to see a dance show in our little town, Lugansk in eastern Ukraine, with many dance styles. The ballroom dancing – with the ladies in beautiful sparkling gowns with feathers, beautiful make-up and hair, dancing so elegantly, and the gentlemen dressed up in the tuxedos – took my breath away. It was LOVE. I was too young to sign up for the dance school, so I had to wait until I was five. After only a few months of dance classes I won a beginners dance competition. From then on, everything was about dancing; I never wanted to do anything else. I'm so grateful I had the support of my parents and that all the dreams I had as a little girl came true. Now I have my little daughter, Mila, who will probably be a dancer herself. So for all the little girls out there, I want to say one thing – please dream and dream big!

Janette Manrara ▶

I started dancing as soon as I could probably walk. Being Cuban, we always had music in the house, mostly Cha-cha-cha and Salsa. I danced standing on my dad's feet at parties, and again with my uncles and grandpas. It was a house where EVERYONE danced! There was always an excuse for it: birthdays, holidays, days off, the weekend!

My first ever dance class was ballet when I was five. My family didn't have money for a leotard, so I wore a pink polka-dot bathing suit. Then they found they couldn't afford the lessons, so that only lasted about three months. I didn't dance again until I was 12, in a musical-theatre school. In that first jazz class, I knew this was something I wanted to do for the rest of my life. That feeling of being lost in a moment with music … it's magical! From that moment on, I decided to live in the magic forever.

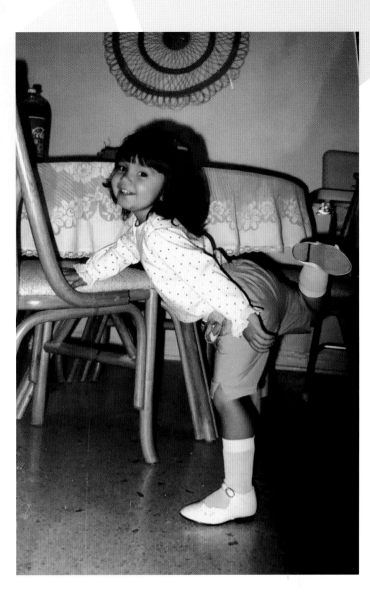

Oti Mabuse

I have two older sisters and I'd been watching them dance for a long time. One day, when I was four, I turned off the TV and was like, 'Right, guys. It's the Oti Show.' I made everyone – my sisters, my mum, my dad – watch me dance, and I was doing all my sisters' Cha-cha-cha routines – and doing it all wrong! So my mum decided I needed to go to dance class.

At class, I was put with this partner who I wasn't happy with, as he kept making excuses and I didn't like his work ethic! When we had our first competition, we were out by the first round and I just cried and told them, 'This is never going to happen again!'

Even though that first competition didn't go well, I knew I loved competitive dancing. I loved the training, the competition, the hair and the make-up. I loved that people supported you and encouraged you too.

I remember thinking, 'I want to do this for the rest of my life, but I want to be the best!' At the next competition I had a new partner – and we won!

▲ Johannes Radebe

I grew up in the South African township of Sasolburg, and back home, everybody dances. We dance at celebrations, and when people are angry they still dance. One day, when I was seven, I was told a dance school was opening up and I was so intrigued. I went to this recreation hall, where a couple were demonstrating what they were going to teach the kids and, cleverly, they wore the full ballroom outfits. The man was wearing a white jacket tailcoat with silver sequins and the lady's dress was off-white, with pink feathers at the bottom. I fell in love with the glamour, because everything sparkled, and I just wanted to be able to wear that jacket. So it wasn't so much the dancing that drew me in!

When I entered my first competition, I realised there's another world, with people who are invested in something. The idea of leaving the township and going to a big city like Johannesburg also had a big appeal and we would travel every weekend to provincial championships too.

I got my first trophy when I was eight, at a big competition that involved all the other provinces. I remember the smile on my mum's face when I came home with my first ever trophy. She couldn't contain her excitement. She put me on her back and, holding the trophy in one hand, she ran to the family to tell them the news. It was not even first prize, but I'd made it to the finals. That moment, seeing my mum so happy, got me going back and wanting to bring more trophies home!

▼ Nancy Xu

I was eight when I started my very first Latin and ballroom class. I didn't even know this kind of dance existed, but I liked the music so much. I saw a group of teenagers performing in front of me and the girls were dressed beautifully. That's the reason I started. It amazed me from the first moment I saw it.

I was always used as the example in the dance class and my teacher would call me out to dance a solo, which gave me the self-confidence for my first competition.

In the beginning I was a bit nervous, but excitement took over when my dance partner and I won two different groups in the biggest competition in the country. This gave me the strength to keep dancing.

▲ Amy Dowden

The first time I danced was in a disco dance competition on holiday in Cornwall. I loved it. The audience, the spotlights and, of course, the fact that I was lucky enough to win. I felt something special I'd never experienced before. After that, my parents took my twin sister and myself to our local dance school. Growing up, all I wanted to do was dance. I would choose my dance lessons over parties, school trips and even holidays. I lived for the nights I was dancing and my Saturday mornings. I loved the lessons, the beautiful dresses, competing and taking my medal tests.

I will never forget when I first walked into the Tower Ballroom in Blackpool, at eight years old. It felt better than Disneyland. It was in a formation team for the Junior British Open Dance Festival and I had to be bribed to leave, I loved it so much. I turned to my mum and said, 'I want to be a professional dancer.'

I counted down the months till April when I would then be returning to the Blackpool Tower Ballroom.

My biggest memory has to be winning the British National Championships with my fiancé in 2017 – all the work I'd put in since I was eight paid off. And, of course, being asked to join the incredible team of *Strictly Come Dancing*.

▼ Graziano di Prima

My mum took me to my first class, in our small home town, at six. I was dancing with my cousin who was smart and was getting the steps really fast while I was messing about and running around. Eventually the teacher said, 'Will you stay still for a second!'

After three weeks, the teacher asked my parents if we could go to our first dance competition. My mum thought it was too soon but the teacher explained, 'It'll be a great experience for them, they should enter as many competitions as they can.' We won the competition and I liked the feeling of winning so I never stopped.

At the time, I loved playing football with the kids out the back of the house but after I started dancing, my mum said, 'You can't go outside to play football because if you break a leg you won't be able to dance anymore.' So I grew up knowing that dancing was the key to my dreams and I found a way to follow my dream. I thank God that my parents were behind me.

Shirley Ballas

With a lifetime of experience as a dancer, teacher and judge, Shirley Ballas is always excited to see a new batch of novices learning their first ballroom and Latin steps.

'I'm ecstatic about the new series, because it's going to be something for people to look forward to,' she says. 'The cast the producers have put together is going to be very entertaining. It's not just about the dancing and the improvements, it's also going to be about their journey, and I think people are really going to get involved in the contestants' stories. Of course, I always love a little humour, and there will be that, too, and I think that we have a broad spectrum of people for the show.'

Head judge Shirley is particularly pleased to see Nicola Adams dancing in the show's first same-sex celebrity–pro partnership.

'I love everybody's journey, but I'm particularly looking forward to watching Nicola because I used to dance with a girl myself, from the age of seven to 12. That's common in the dance world, where a class might have 20 girls to one boy. In the industry, in Blackpool, we have both male and female partnerships. When I judge them, I'm judging footwork and musicality. For me, it's just movement to music and it's not gender-oriented.'

Shirley also has a word of encouragement for Jamie Laing, back for a second time after being forced to withdraw with an injury last year.

'He will have an amazing time and it's the honourable thing to do, to give him a second shot,' she says. 'The new series is the new series and there's no comparing to the last one. Every single person has their own journey and that's what makes each and every one unique.'

Strictly's own Queen of Latin started dancing at the age of seven and remains the only person to have won the British Open and the World Latin American Championships in Blackpool with two different partners. Before joining the Strictly panel she had already become an international coach and sought-after judge. Last year, she was delighted to welcome friend and colleague Motsi Mabuse and says she adds something special to the judging panel.

'Motsi is an absolute breath of fresh air and we're completely on the same page,' she says. 'We stay in touch, on and off the show. She brings everything that is fun, that is educated, and she's uplifting to be around.

'We are the Fab Four, because we have so much fun! It's a laugh a minute and Motsi enhances that. She brings out the best in everybody.

'I can't wait to see the other judges, but I'll miss Bruno as my "left-hand man". I'll even miss dodging his arms when he gets overenthusiastic.'

Raring to go for the new series, Shirley promises it will be every bit as fabulous as the last, which saw late arrival Kelvin Fletcher sweep to victory.

'Mike Bushell was one of my favourites because he represented everything that Strictly is about – fun, hard-working, keen to get it right.

'But the series-17 Final was absolutely off the chart. For somebody who hadn't danced before, Kelvin was spectacular. I wondered how they were going to top it, but that's the beauty of the show. Just when you think it couldn't get any better, it does, and this year will be the best yet. We all need a little bit of Hollywood glitz, glamour, baubles, bangles and beads, and we will get all that in spades.'

Bill Bailey

As a comedian, Bill Bailey is used to physically demanding live shows, but he has also taken part in a range of extreme hobbies, including paddle boarding, jet water biking, quad biking, paintballing and cycling. So he is relishing the physical challenge of *Strictly Come Dancing*.

'One of the great draws of the show is staying active and learning a new skill,' he says. 'Being able to work with the professionals, who are extraordinary, is a privilege. They've dedicated their lives to this and to have the opportunity to tap into that knowledge, that experience and that skill is a wonderful treat.'

Bath-born Bill began his stand-up career in 1984, before landing his first TV show, *Is It Bill Bailey?*, in 1998. He went on to star in *Black Books* and served as a team captain on *Never Mind the Buzzcocks*, as well as making frequent appearances on panel shows including *QI* and *Have I Got News For You*. Having signed up for *Strictly,* Bill is keen to go all the way.

'Obviously, it would be amazing if I was able to continue through the competition, mainly because you improve exponentially as you go on,' he says. 'The experience is new, the physicality of it is new, but you learn what's required, and then you improve and get through to the next week. That gives you more confidence, so it's a positive loop.'

To help him achieve that, Bill wants a professional partner who will keep pushing him to his limit. 'I want someone who doesn't pull any punches and isn't going to sugar-coat it,' he says. 'I need someone to tell it straight. They will need a degree of patience too, although I'm a quick learner, this is like a whole new language to me. I want to be pushed to keep practising until I get it right. As someone who's learning, I want to put 100 per cent in so I can give a good account of myself.'

As well as being an award-winning comic and documentary maker, Bill is a talented musician who has played in many bands and incorporates music into his live tours. Now he's hoping that dancing may play a part in future shows.

'I recently started archiving 25 years of my live performances and I was amazed to find that, in almost every show, there was some element of choreographed movement – I wouldn't call it dance,' he jokes. 'If you're on stage for two and a half hours, you have to have lots of different elements, and dance is the one element that I haven't properly explored. Hopefully, this show is a way to inspire me to do more of that.'

He is also looking forward to expanding his wardrobe choices for the show. 'I've worn all manner of stuff, and I secretly love dressing up and putting on spangly stuff,' he says. 'When I was looking at what to wear to my first day on the *Strictly* set, I came across a suit which I had made for my *Tinselworm* arena tour. It's heavily embroidered, with rhinestones all over, so it's very *Strictly*. Clearly, this is something which has been percolating away for a while.'

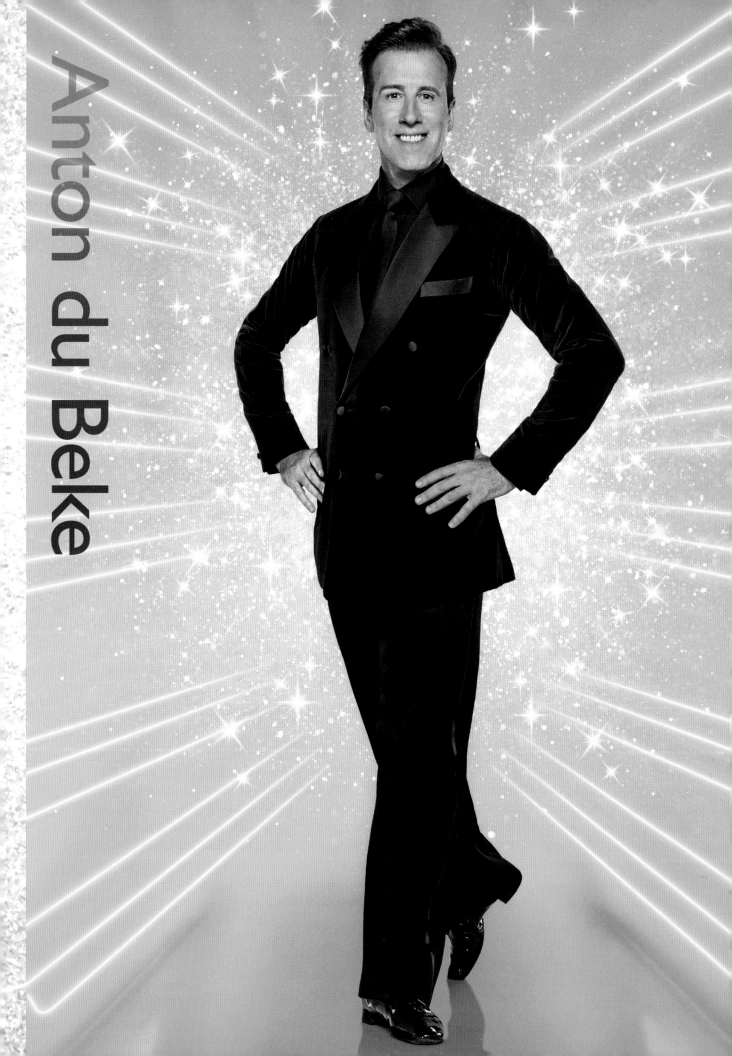

Anton du Beke

Last year was special for ballroom king Anton du Beke, who reached the final dancing with *EastEnders* star Emma Barton. The couple notched up a score of 39 for their Charleston and 39 for their final Viennese Waltz.

'You know the old adage, seventeenth time lucky,' he jokes. 'Last year was a vintage year, the best of all years. It was a year of firsts and I got my first 10, for our Waltz, so that was brilliant.'

Anton, the only professional to have been with the show since the beginning, says he and Emma combined hard work with a great deal of fun throughout the series.

'We have a very similar sense of humour and we're sort of cut from the same cloth,' he says. 'So we did mess about quite a lot, but we both loved what we were doing, we both love the style of dancing. When I was choreographing the dance I didn't just make up a routine and then hand it to Emma; we came up with it together, which was lovely. She is a hard worker and a pro. Plus, she was a huge *Strictly Come Dancing* fan and was so happy to be there – she enjoyed every minute.'

Anton was visibly moved on the show by their elegant week-12 Waltz to Gymnopédie No.1 by Erik Satie, which saw Bruno award the coveted 10. He told the judges, 'This is somebody who had no confidence in her dancing ability, didn't think she could dance a step, to make it into the Semi-finals as well. And to produce a dance like that, that I've been wanting to do for 16 years on *Strictly Come Dancing*, is the most beautiful thing.'

Anton was born in Sevenoaks, Kent, to a Spanish mother and Hungarian father. A junior boxer and county footballer, he started dancing at the relatively late age of 14, studying contemporary, jazz, ballet and modern theatre dance. At 17, Anton chose to specialise in ballroom, favouring the Foxtrot, after being inspired by his idol, Fred Astaire.

To pay his way he got a job as a bed salesman at 17, training and competing in the evenings and at weekends.

In 1997, Anton met Erin Boag, and within a year the duo had become New Zealand champions, successfully defending their title the following year. The pair joined *Strictly* for the first series in 2004 when Anton made the Final with opera star Lesley Garrett. Since then Anton has partnered 16 celebrities, including Lesley Joseph, Ruth Langsford and Esther Rantzen. He has also produced many of the show's most iconic moments – from Ann Widdecombe's *Titanic* Rumba to Judy Murray's Cruella de Vil American Smooth and Nancy Dell'Olio's Halloween Rumba. In 2015, Anton made it to the Grand Final for the first time in 12 series, with Radio 3 presenter Katie Derham, coming fourth in the competition.

As well as a host of 10s last year, Anton got his first ever spray tan!

'With the clothes I wear I normally have a light dusting on my face, but last year I went for the full facial spray tan. A full body tan would be a waste of bedsheets!'

This year, Anton is hoping he will finally get his hands on the elusive glitterball. But whatever happens, he is delighted to be back in his dancing shoes for another series and ready to wow the *Strictly* viewers with his amazing routines.

'I think there'll be a desire for it this year because it is a wonderful thing,' he says. 'It is a wonderfully uplifting show and a show of positivity – apart from Craig Revel Horwood, of course. So I think we're all ready for a bit of that.'

STRICTLY STYLE

The Paso Doble and the Tango are among the most intense dances in the *Strictly Come Dancing* repertoire, and they demand a dramatic look.

Here, Make-Up Designer Lisa Armstrong and Hair Designer Lisa Davey reveal the secrets behind two of their personal favourites from the last two years.

Lisa Davey's choice

EMMA BARTON'S HALLOWEEN TANGO

Lisa Armstrong says: 'The Queen-of-Hearts look that we created for Emma Barton is one of my favourite Halloween looks of all time, and I love that Anton mirrored her as the King of Clubs.

'We wanted to make it quirky, not cute. More from Tim Burton's *Alice in Wonderland* than Disney's.

'We drew the heart across one of her eyes, freehand, using lip liner. It was really difficult because it's not a flat surface and you have an eye socket, the bridge of a nose and a cheekbone. It has to be symmetrical because I'm obsessive when it comes to attention to detail, so I can't have a wonky heart!

'We drew the outline and filled it in with a lip pencil. I didn't want to use shadow because there's too much droppage and I needed something that glitter would stick to.

'Once the heart was finished, my assistant and I painstakingly stuck individual crystals around the eye, using eyelash glue, to make the colour pop. I don't think either of us breathed for half an hour!

'Then we cleaned up everything around the heart, and started work on the 'pretty eye', starting with the base and blending the red colour, then adding the black liner and the lash.

'When we'd finished, the heart eye looked really strong and powerful, but we were losing the other eye, so I needed to balance it in some way. Coincidentally, I had bought some heart-shaped confetti – the sort you sprinkle on tables at birthday

parties – so suddenly it came to me that I could stick that all around the other eye.

'We alternated between the right way up and upside down, all round her eye with eyelash glue – and it looked amazing. Emma loved that look.

'With Anton, I decided to hand-draw a King-of-Clubs playing card over the side of his eye, so he mirrored Emma's Queen of Hearts.

'The quirky look gave a hidden depth to the deck-of-cards theme – the almighty king and the feisty queen. What's great with *Strictly* is that we can be so creative and give the look underlying meaning, which viewers may or may not pick up on. That's what makes it the best job in the world!'

Lisa Davey says: 'As soon as I knew the concept of the look, I came up with the image of how I wanted the hair to be. As always, we then had a creative meeting with production in Halloween Week to make sure everyone was happy, then the image was passed on to the team member that would be creating the look – in this case, stylist Georgia Woodland.

'Emma's wig was actually recycled and had previously been worn by Kate Silverton, when she was dancing as Jessica Rabbit.

'The beauty of using a wig is that we can work on it and prep it during the week, ready for show day.

'We slightly changed the colour and added extra hair extensions, plus padding and accessories, to create the striking conical shapes for the Queen of Hearts. With the costume and make-up, the whole look was amazing.'

Lisa Armstrong's choice

STACEY DOOLEY'S PASO DOBLE

Lisa Armstrong says: 'When Stacey first came in she was the girl next door who didn't want any heavy make-up – just a flick of mascara and some lip balm. We had to gain her trust, but by week 3 we had her dressed as a Minion, painted yellow, with goggles on her head and coat hangers in her hair! She embraced the whole journey of *Strictly*.

'For her week-10 Paso I told her, "I'm going to go dark, dark, dark on you!" She was unsure, but she was willing to let me try, and I promised her we would take it off if she didn't like it. That's the beauty of what we create: it can be changed, and we want to make people feel comfortable.

'In her Paso with Kevin, Stacey is the forceful one and I knew dark black eyes would add so much drama against her beautiful English-rose skin.

'I mixed a really dark brown eyeshadow and blended it into black, then added dark black liner and thick, black lashes with a prominent arched brow.

'To make sure the eyes were striking and dramatic, we kept the rest of the face really clean. Her skin tone was pale, with no highlighter, no bronzer, no sparkle or glitter. Then I went over her mouth with foundation, let her lips breathe a bit and then just patted a hint of lip balm on them, and that completed the look.

'There was so much drama going on in the eyes, with all that passion and intensity, a heavy lip would have spoilt it. Sometimes less is more.

'I think that look helped Stacey get into her character, She went from the usual lovely, fun, bubbly Stacey to a strong, powerful, all-eyes-on-me Stacey.'

Lisa Davey says: 'Stacey Dooley's Paso hairstyle was basically a ponytail, because I wanted it to be simple yet dramatic! The look also has to represent the powerful, no-nonsense style of the dance.

'Her hair was parted in the centre and slicked down, then we banded it at the nape.

'A longer hair piece was attached to create length and drama, and a band of black leather fabric was wrapped around it from the nape of her neck to halfway down the pony tail, then stitched to keep it safely in place. The finished look was striking and fitted the drama of the Paso perfectly.'

Jason Bell

After a long and distinguished career in American football, Jason Bell believes his time in the NFL (National Football League) has left him with transferable skills for his stint on *Strictly*.

'In football, my position was all about footwork,' he says. 'When I went out with friends, I'd be on the dance floor and really working on football moves and footwork, so it goes hand in hand. I've always danced and I enjoy it as entertainment.'

As a sportsman, Jason is used to long hours of training, which will serve him well as he learns the routines, and he's got a strong competitive streak. But he's not eyeing up his competition on the dance floor.

'I don't think like that because of my sports background,' he says. 'Whenever you say you're in a competition for a position on a team, you can get really caught up with how the other guy is doing and it impacts your performance. So I just focus on what I have got to do, because that's the only thing I can control.'

Born in California, Jason won a sports scholarship at UCLA before going on to play for the Dallas Cowboys, Houston Texans and New York Giants. He retired in 2008 and is now a businessman and respected NFL pundit. He's relishing the new challenge of dancing on *Strictly*, which he says he accepted because it made him nervous.

'I've always challenged myself – sport has forced that,' he says. 'But when I retired and started other ventures, everything I was scared of, I took that challenge on and I've learned something from it. I've learned about myself and how I operate. You only get that when you put yourself in an uncomfortable position, *Strictly* will be a challenge on every level. I don't like being the centre of attention. Having to learn a new skill, compete and be judged by the best is a lot of pressure, but I think I'm going to hone some skills that I don't know I have yet.'

Another reason he is excited to take part is for his daughter, six-year-old Anaíya, who he shares with singer Nadine Coyle and is a big fan of the show. And Nadine is giving him plenty of dance advice.

'Both Nadine and Anaíya have been super supportive,' says Jason. 'They're as excited as I am, and they talk about it every day. My daughter can't wait and tells me how nervous she is going to be, and I talk to Nadine all the time about how to prepare for dance routines because she's a walking expert, so I'm lucky. Having their support is the key and I really just want to go out there and represent them well, because they mean so much to me.'

Jason has also been given a sound piece of advice from a friend who competed in *Dancing with the Stars* in the US. 'It was probably one of the best tips I could have heard and it was to trust your professional, listen to them. Don't try to go out there and learn on your own. They are the best teachers in the world, so give them a blank canvas.'

As well as learning a new skill, Jason is excited about meeting his fellow contestants.

'I think the group is very diverse, which I love,' he says. 'It has people from all different walks of life and I love meeting people and being on a team with people from different backgrounds, ages, genders, etc. I have got a bunch of new best friends and I'm excited to engage with all of them because they seem so cool.'

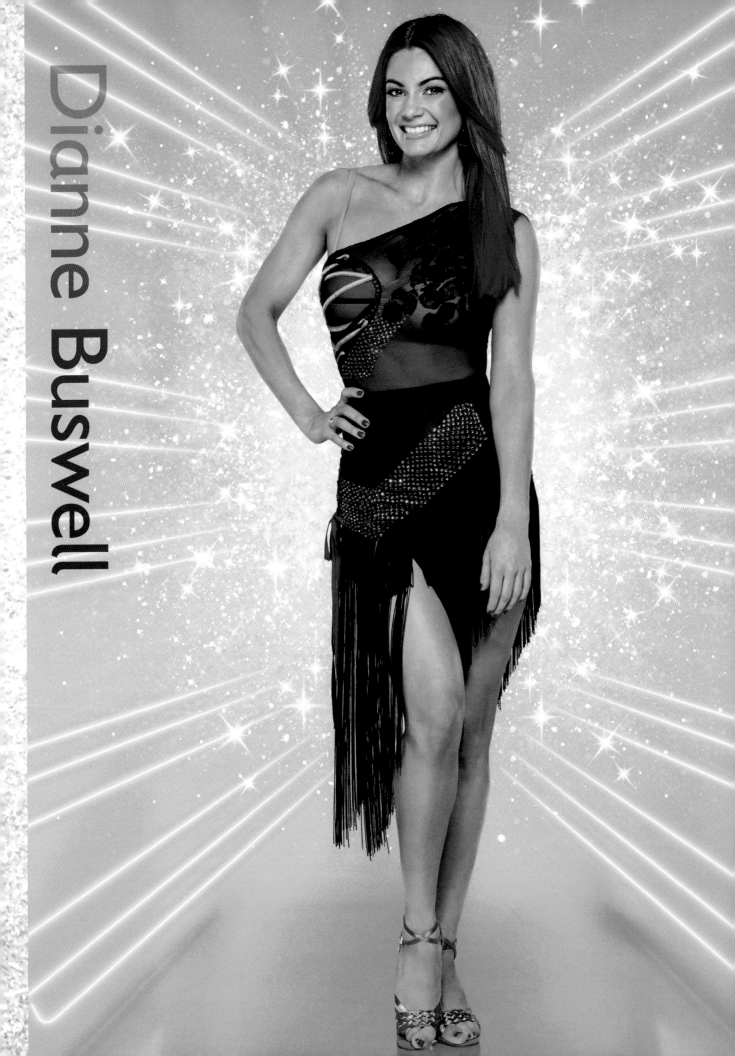

Dianne Buswell

Former finalist Dianne Buswell is more than ready to hit the dance floor running when this series of Strictly kicks off. 'I can't wait to get into the sparkle of Strictly again,' she says. 'It's something that instantly makes you smile, so I'm looking forward to us all being together and dancing.'

Getting back into rehearsals with the group dancers after an eight-month break from the show is exciting for all. 'It's amazing to be back,' she says. 'It felt like coming home.

'Dusting off the dancing shoes was a wonderful feeling. Also waking up with my body aching a little, after the first full day of dance, is something I love.'

In the run-up to the new season, the Australian professional has been putting some ideas together and promises a few surprises.

'I've been able to work on things and get creative and I've had time to think outside the box,' she says. 'This year, I definitely want to push the boundaries with my choreography – so watch out for that.'

An Australian Open Champion and four-time Amateur Australian Open Finalist, Dianne was a professional dancer on the Australian version of Strictly Come Dancing before joining the UK series in 2017, when she partnered the Reverend Richard Coles. The following year, she reached the Final with social-media star Joe Sugg and, in series 17, she partnered BBC Radio 1 DJ Dev Griffin.

'I loved working with Dev,' she says. 'He's such a talented guy and an absolute dream to teach. We enjoyed every moment. I particularly loved our Street/Commercial dance to "Friend Like Me" from Aladdin, where we played the Genie and Abu. They are such great characters, the music was perfect and the costumes were amazing, so everything clicked. That was really special, but Dev performed all our routines really well and I was so proud of him. We're still friends and I know he's going to be rooting for me this year.'

Dianne believes dancing is a superb way to get people moving and to improve mental health.

'Not everybody enjoys running on a treadmill or going on a 5k run,' she says. 'Dancing is an exercise that's joyful and you don't feel like you're exercising, because you're having so much fun. A lot of young girls have messaged me saying, "If it wasn't for dance I'd probably not be doing any form of exercise."

'Getting your body moving is also a huge boost for mental health. Just moving a little bit can change your mood and send endorphins through your body. If I wake up and have a bit of a down day, dancing and moving my body really helps.'

With a few months on the Strictly dance floor ahead, Dianne couldn't be happier, and she's thrilled that loyal viewers will get their annual fix of sparkle in the run-up to Christmas. 'The response we've had from viewers is that they are so excited to have Strictly back,' she says. 'It's such a big part of this country and it's so nice that we've been able to make the magic of Strictly happen – not only for us, but for all the fans out there. They're delighted and I'm just as excited as they are.'

SCRIBBLY COME DANCING

As well as being amazing dancers, many of the pros on *Strictly* harbour hidden talents as artists. For this fun quiz, they have taken a stab at drawing one of their fellow dancers, so can you guess who is in each picture? There's a bonus point for each one if you can guess who the secret artist is …

5

6

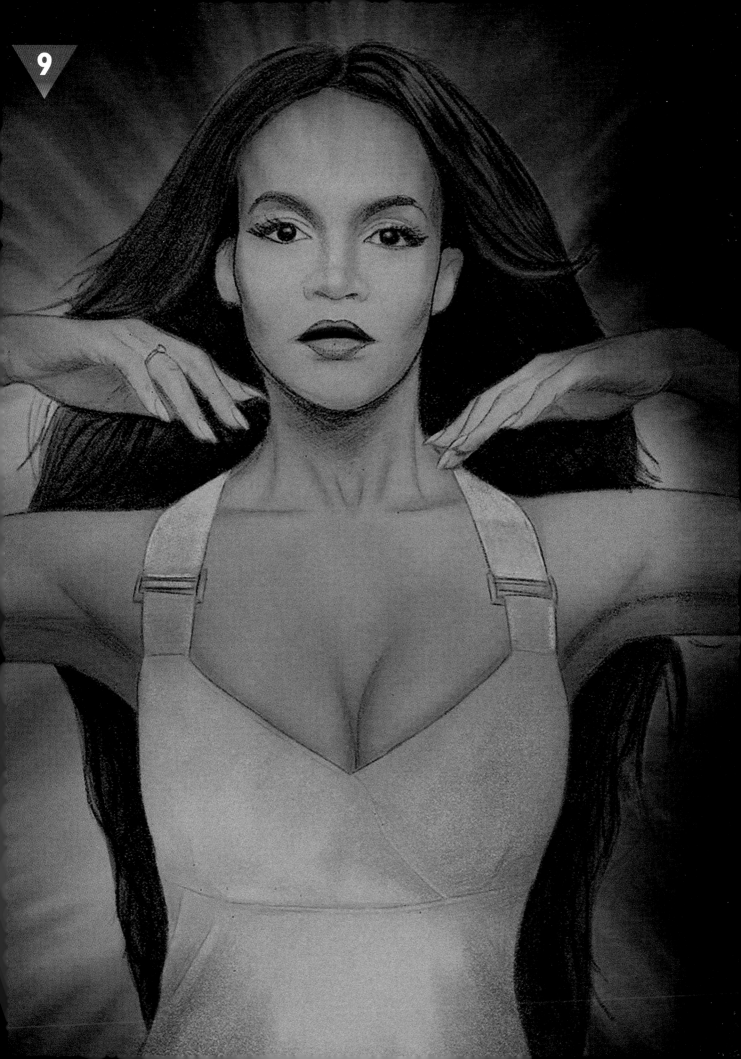

Craig Revel Horwood

Craig Revel Horwood has been keeping *Strictly* fans amused since series 1 – as well as earning himself the odd boo. But the straight-talking judge, who rarely digs out his 10 paddle, is looking forward to being entertained when the couples take to the dance floor this year.

'I'm very much excited about coming back and seeing all the dancing,' he says. 'As well as being wonderful for fans, it's entertainment for me. It means I get out of the house and see a show, and I have a front-row seat – so I'm one of the lucky ones.'

What do you think of the line-up this year?

It looks good and I think it's going to be great fun. I'm especially pleased to see Jamie Laing coming back. It was so sad when he had to leave last year because of injury, so it is really nice to know that he's coming back and getting a second opportunity to prove his worth. I'm looking forward to seeing Nicola Adams in the same-sex couple. I'm also looking forward to meeting Caroline Quentin, because I think she'll be fantastic in the show, but I'm excited about all of them.

Will you miss Bruno sitting with you in the studio?

Oh, of course I'll miss Bruno! But we'll still be hearing his dulcet tones, and we're hoping he'll be there with us for the final two [shows], as it would be so good to have him back for that explosion of glamour on the Semi-final and Grand Final.

What did Motsi bring to the panel in her first year as a UK judge?

Motsi was really great. We get on so well. It is fun sitting next to someone so bubbly and bouncy, plus she knows her stuff. She's done nine years on the version of *Strictly Come Dancing* in Germany, so she knows what she's doing, and it's going to be fantastic to have her back for the second time.

What did you make of last year's Final?

All three contestants were amazing, and it was wonderful to see Anton du Beke in the Final. I loved the fact that Kelvin won because he was the dark horse, a late entry, and he absolutely smashed it. He's probably the biggest surprise winner we've ever had. When you see someone that muscular, you don't expect them to dance, but he was footloose and fancy free and it was amazing. A well-deserved winner.

What were your favourite dances of last year?

There were many memorable moments and as always, I loved all the show dances. What sticks in the memory for me though is that the Charlestons were really good, because everyone had really worked on their swivel, which was amazing. I've been banging on about the swivel – the technical side of the dance – for years and last year people buckled down and made it work. So I was delighted with that!

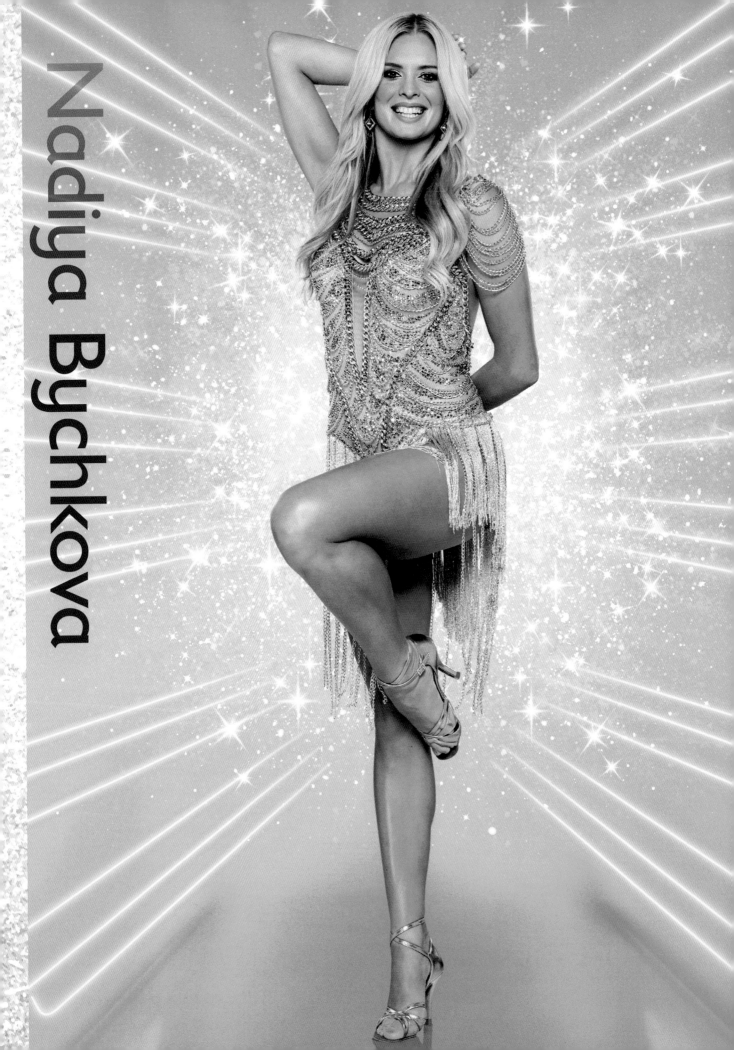

Nadiya Bychkova

Ukrainian pro Nadiya Bychkova is excited to be returning for her fourth series and she's looking forward to the group numbers with her fellow dancers.

'I'm really happy we are back for another series,' she says. 'I don't know how it's possible but every year I say it's the best show we've ever had, and this year we have taken the dances to a different level and they are just incredible. There is one very special number, for me, where I have the lead and it's a very classy routine, like a little movie. But all the routines are just amazing.'

The 16 professional dancers are a close-knit group and gel on and off the dance floor, says Nadiya. 'We have kept in contact throughout the last eight months and I think our connection is one of the things that has taken us to an even higher level of performance this year. Now we're back in rehearsals, we can be focused and concentrate on producing amazing numbers, and the bond between all of us helps to create something incredible. I just can't wait for the fans to see the dances. It's going to be beautiful.'

Born in Lugansk, Nadiya trained at the same Slovenian dance school as Aljaž Škorjanec and won the Slovenian Ballroom and Latin Championship multiple times as well as being two-time World Champion and European Champion in ballroom and Latin Ten Dance. She joined the show in 2017, making

it to the Quarter-finals with actor Davood Ghadami. Most recently, she made it to week five with footballer David James.

'It was an amazing experience,' she says. 'He's an athlete and has an athlete's mind, so long hours weren't a problem. He's a really focused man and very dedicated. When he started he was saying. "I'm not a dancer, there's no way I can be good." But I managed to convince him he could and, week by week, he was getting better. He was starting to believe in himself, and that's what Strictly Come Dancing is all about – finding your new limits and learning something you never thought you were capable of.'

As the new contestants prepare to take to the floor for this series, Nadiya wants them to make the most of their Strictly journey. 'It's such a unique experience and the celebrities should take it all in, second by second, minute by minute and performance by performance. Looking at the line-up, the competition will be tough, but getting a chance to do Strictly is incredible. Enjoy it, make the most of it and make it fun.'

She also has some advice when it comes to dealing with the judges' comments. 'What they say is usually positive and you can always learn from it. Take their advice, try to do your best every time and remember that just to be on the show and being able to do something which is out of your comfort zone – it's already a huge achievement. You should be proud of yourselves.'

JJ Chalmers

Since sustaining devastating injuries in Afghanistan in 2011, former Marine JJ Chalmers has learned to scuba dive, won a gold medal for cycling in the Invictus Games and become a TV presenter. Now he is approaching his latest challenge with the same fearless attitude.

'Believe it or not, all of the things I've done before, including Afghanistan, I enjoyed,' he says. 'First and foremost, I went there to do my job, proudly. Even throughout my recovery, I did it with a smile on my face, so I want to come to *Strictly* and enjoy the process, but I'm also here to work hard. This is an unbelievable opportunity to learn a new skill with the very best in the business and that's what really excited me about this. So I'm going to be eating, sleeping and breathing *Strictly*, because I want to give this the best crack I possibly can.'

Trained as a teacher, JJ Chalmers was a Marine reservist when he was sent to the Helmand Province. In May 2011, his patrol was searching a bomb factory when an IED exploded. 'I was incredibly badly injured and over months and years surgeons re-built my body and I then spent the best part of five years learning how to use that body. Now we're going to find out if it's fixed or not. That's the amazing thing about this process.'

Although he feels there are some moves that he will struggle with, JJ says he wants his professional partner to help him find his 'new limitations'.

'I very much doubt I'm going to be able to go full Patrick Swayze and hold my partner in the air, because I can barely lift my arms above my head,' he says. 'I'm going to be sensible and listen to my body, but I'm excited about doing eight hours of physical activity a day, which I haven't done since training for the Invictus Games and the Marines. There are not many better forms of activity than dancing for improving your overall body posture, fitness and mobility. I'm hoping I go as far as I possibly can, because I want to see the benefit and come out more able than I've ever been.'

JJ has little when it comes to dance experience, but incredibly, before he was injured, he was learning the Waltz from a colleague who is a familiar name to *Strictly* fans.

'I was meant to be coming back to be at my brother's wedding in the halfway point in the military tour, and our medic, Cassidy Little, had been a semi-professional dancer before he joined the Marines. He was teaching me how to waltz so I could impress my girlfriend, now wife, with my moves. The two of us were in shorts in the middle of nowhere, in 40-degree heat, learning the dance. Unfortunately, both of us were blown up in the same incident, and Cassidy lost his leg. But he went on to win *The People's Strictly for Comic Relief*.'

As a tough ex-military man, JJ says he can handle the judges' feedback.

'I hope that the critique pushes me more,' he says. 'The judges, and everybody in this process, only want the best for the individual. They want to see the best performances, and for the viewers to have the best experience. If you don't get that feedback, how can you ever improve?'

After spending a chunk of his life in uniform, JJ's not afraid of donning the sparkle either. 'I'm here to immerse myself in this process,' he says. 'If you're not embracing it fully then you're wasting an opportunity, if you're not glammed up, you're the odd one out!'

STRICTLY GOES GREEN

Glitter and shimmer are an integral part of ballroom's glamour and synonymous with *Strictly Come Dancing*. But over the last few years, *Strictly* has been going green – ensuring that the famous sparkles look as good as ever but don't end up damaging the environment.

From 2018, all loose glitter powder used in the iconic looks is sourced from specialist environmentally friendly suppliers, and is 100 per cent biodegradable, meaning it poses no threat to marine life if washed down the sink. All the make-up used in the show is also biodegradable and the wipes used to remove it are eco-friendly.

But the changes go far beyond the beauty products used by the make-up department.

The special effects that provide the routine with extra wow factor – from fireworks to confetti showers – are now 95 per cent biodegradable.

The props that set the scene for each dance are stored away once the routine is over, to be reused or recycled later.

Single-use plastic bottles have been eradicated on set, with cast and crew switching to refillable water bottles instead. The catering company, which serves the cast and crew with lunch and dinner in the Star Bar, now uses exclusively sustainable products, including wooden cutlery, recyclable takeaway boxes and compostable cups.

The generators that supply electricity to the studio have been switched to plant-based biofuel, which cuts out the need to burn fossil fuels and reduces carbon dioxide emissions.

Even the taxis to and from the studio are taken into account, with only low-emission cabs now being used by the production.

This year also marks the third series in which camera operators have used tablets for their shot cards (the documents that tell them which camera is taking each shot throughout the routines).

Strictly led the way in replacing the reams of paper that used to be printed off for each camera, switching to the new technology in 2017.

'We used to have paper shot cards that we wrote our own notes on,' says Camera Supervisor Lincoln Abraham. 'Now we use tablets and we have the facility to make notes on the cards on screen, which cuts down on a lot of paper wastage.

'It took a while, but we all got used to them and we love the system now. Hopefully, we are helping the environment every way we can.'

In 2019, Production Executive Kate Jones began investigating a carbon-offset scheme, which is currently awaiting approval.

'We are proud to be a sustainable production and continue to review our green initiatives throughout the series,' says Kate.

As a result of all the changes over recent years, *Strictly* is now certified by the BAFTA Albert scheme, which recognises shows that have cut their carbon footprints.

That's an achievement worthy of a glitterball trophy.

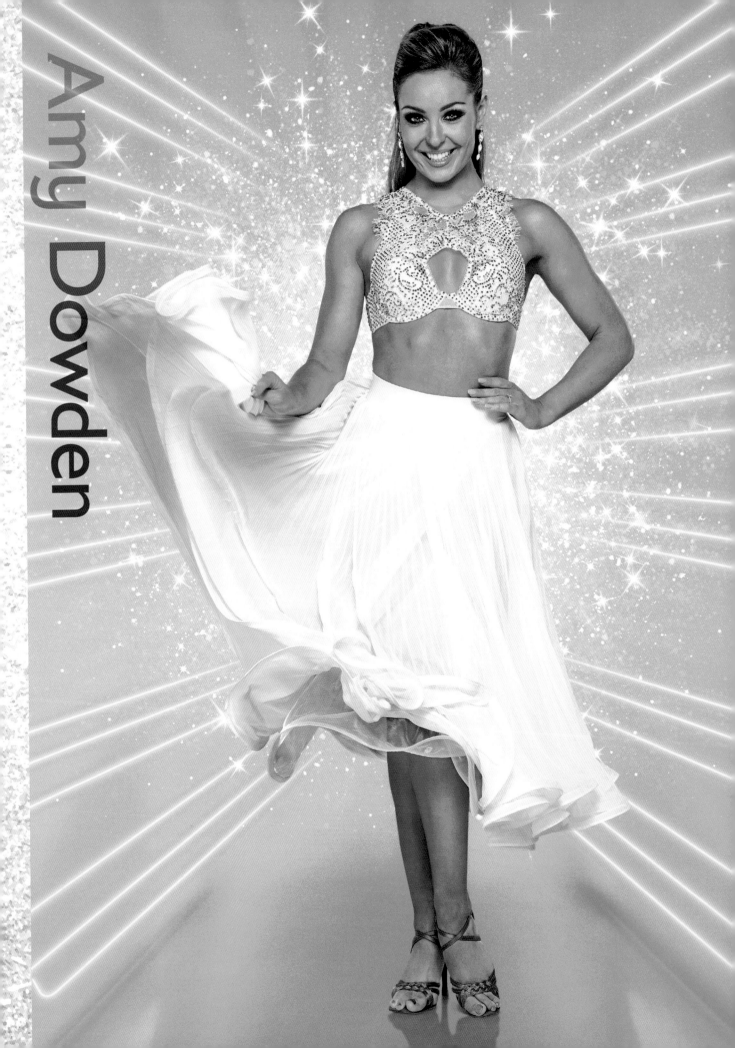

Amy Dowden

Former finalist Amy Dowden has been watching *Strictly Come Dancing* since she was a child and says the start of each series puts her in a festive mood.

'*Strictly* is a real family show and always brings a feeling of happiness,' she says. 'It's a little bit of magic, especially for me, because I've been a fan for years and years. Even before I joined the show.'

Born and raised in Caerphilly, Amy began dancing at the age of eight and is a four-time British National Finalist and a British National Champion, making her one of the highest-ranking ballroom and Latin dancers in the UK. As a long-time viewer, Amy saw her dream of dancing on *Strictly* come true when she joined in 2017, and she says coming back to rehearsals and seeing her fellow pros at the start of each season is still a special moment.

'It's just a pure joy to be back together and doing what we love and hopefully creating more magic for the season,' she says. 'The first day in group rehearsals is exciting and emotional. Everyone is absolutely buzzing and can't wait to get stuck into training.'

As well as the couples' dances, Amy says viewers are in for a treat when it comes to the spectacular group numbers planned for this series.

'I'm so excited about each and every number,' she says. 'The group dance is the start of the show to me and gives the nation a taste of what's to come from the other dances. As dancers, we love to test ourselves, and Jason Gilkison, our Creative Director, always amazes us with his concepts and his choreography. He pushes us all to be better dancers and I love just being around my fellow pros. I feel they make me more creative as well.'

In 2019, Amy was paired with CBBC presenter Karim Zeroual, receiving the first 40 of the series and a place in its Final.

'I remember being with Karim backstage just before we walked down the stairs and hearing "Live from London. This is the Grand Final of *Strictly Come Dancing*." We were literally jumping up and down with excitement,' she recalls. 'I turned to him and said, "Just enjoy every beat on that dance floor."

'My parents were in the audience, but I couldn't look at them because I would have cried. I was so proud of him and if I could relive that Final I would in a flash. I genuinely loved every second. For Karim and me, it was the icing on the cake to be in the Final and we really felt like we'd won the glitterball already.'

Karim, she says, was a model pupil, combining talent and enthusiasm in equal measure.

'Karim just oozes rhythm,' she says. 'He was an absolute dream to work with and we're still really good friends now.'

Amy is looking forward to meeting the next batch of willing pupils in the *Strictly* class of 2020.

'It's a brilliant line-up this year,' she says. 'I'm really excited about meeting all the celebrities and watching them progress as dancers, which is always amazing.'

Max George

As a member of The Wanted, Max George is following in the footsteps of Jay McGuiness, who lifted the glitterball in 2015. But he says his bandmate's victory won't pile on the pressure.

'Jay was always the top dancer,' he says. 'In the audition process for the band, I nearly didn't get in because of dancing and, if we ever did any staging or movement, Jay was the one who choreographed that. So I wouldn't say there's pressure, because I always looked up to Jay in that sense. I won't be comparing myself, but if he can give me any tips, then great.'

Mancunian Max started his musical career in The Avenue, appearing on *The X Factor*, before beating thousands of hopefuls to become one of five members of The Wanted in 2009. The boyband went on to sell over two million UK singles, including two number ones, 'All Time Low' and 'Glad You Came', and three hit albums. Since the band split in 2014, Max has branched out into acting, appearing in several films as well as landing the role of Clint in *Glee*. But he believes his experience in music videos and on the US musical series will be little help when it comes to the live Saturday-night show.

'The advantage of doing pop videos is that you get several takes from different angles, and The Wanted didn't dance in many videos,' he says. 'In one, "All Time Low", we sort of did a quick squat at the same time. On *Glee*, we'd have one day of rehearsal and then would film, but again, it was 30 or 40 takes and I remember one lift which I just couldn't get. I nearly dropped one of the dancers that I was working with and I had to catch her by the face, which wasn't cool. After that they got a body double for the more difficult moves!'

The singer and songwriter says his main competition on the dance floor is 'all 11 of the other contestants' and says he can't wait to get to know them. But he is particularly pleased about one of the 2020 intake.

'I'm absolutely buzzing that Caroline Quentin is here,' he says. 'I'm a huge fan of hers. My brother and I had a massive crush on her when we used to watch *Men Behaving Badly*, but I have been talking to her and she's so cool. She's just class. I already feel so much better about any nerves knowing that she's here.'

In a bid to improve through the series, Max says he is ready to take the judges' criticisms on the chin, as well as their scores.

'Anything around six and above, I'll be buzzing,' he says. 'But anything below that, I'll know I have got some serious work to do. They're there to help and that's part of the show.'

As his family are fans of *Strictly*, Max says they will be glued to the TV on Saturday night, willing him on.

'It's the show that my family all love and have watched for years,' he says. 'I know it's going to be a massive challenge for me because I'm not a dancer, but I'm really excited. I can't wait to get started.'

Tess Daly

'I can't wait,' she says. 'It's a really eclectic bunch this year and on paper they look very exciting.'

Ahead of the launch show, Tess has been casting her eye over the class of 2020 and believes that every one of the celebrities brings a unique ingredient to the *Strictly* mix.

'HRVY has an adoring legion of teenage fans, over 10 million on social media, and my teenage daughter informs me he's the most-followed star in *Strictly* history. His mum is so excited that she will be able to watch him every Saturday night and know where he is! I thought that was lovely.

'Max George is a singer-songwriter from The Wanted and there are always high expectations for boyband members. His own bandmate, Jay McGuiness, is a *Strictly* champ, so he's feeling the pressure and there's plenty of banter going on between him and his mates in the band.

'From what I've heard, Jason Bell, our NFL star, is relishing the chance to train. Former sports stars tend to miss the routine of training, so I think he will adapt well to an eight-hour-plus training day. He wants his six-year-old daughter to watch him because it's her favourite TV show and she's too young to have seen him play in the NFL.

'JJ Chalmers is a former Royal Marine and has competed in the Invictus Games, so he's competitive and used to performing under pressure. I have high hopes for JJ. It's a shame Prince Harry isn't in the country so he could come along and cheer his pal on, but I'm sure he will from afar.'

Last year *Made in Chelsea* star Jamie Laing sustained a tendon injury and had to drop out after the launch show, so Tess is thrilled to have him back.

'Jamie said his mum was so disappointed that she never saw him dance, so he's doing it for her. It must have been pretty hard to sit out the first live show, seeing Kelvin Fletcher Samba up a storm. But he's back and he's determined to prove himself. Welcome back, Jamie, and good luck. I won't say break a leg!'

For entertainment value, Tess thinks Bill Bailey will be a hard act to beat.

'Bill will be one to watch for, hopefully, all the right reasons,' she says. 'He'll be unmissable telly, because he's a laugh a minute. He's a man of many talents – comedian, actor, musician and author. It seems he can turn his hand to anything. But will we be adding dancing to that list?'

When it comes to the ladies, Tess has spotted a lot of potential. 'Clara Amfo is a DJ, with great musicality,' she says. 'so I'm expecting great things. Maisie Smith danced with Kevin Clifton for Children in Need last year and won, so she's proved she's got the moves. But for anyone who feels that is an unfair advantage, she only trained for three hours before that show. She's one to watch.

'Caroline Quentin can act the roles and bring some comedy to the dance floor, so on paper she's already qualified. I hope her feet comply.'

While many of the cast are complete dance novices, there's no lack of commitment and enthusiasm. 'Jacqui Smith, the former Home Secretary, is very brave because this is definitely not her comfort zone,' says Tess. 'She said she last danced 50 years ago when she won the bronze medal for Scottish Highland dancing, but she'll be pushing herself hard.

'Ranvir Singh says she feels like she's on a scary rollercoaster, but once the show starts, she thinks it will be joyful, and she can't wait to be dressed up and *Strictly*-fied.

'Nicola Adams is already making *Strictly* history and I can't wait to watch her in action. I have seen some of her social-media videos and she has a signature move, where she dips her hip, but her professional partner will soon have that trained out of her!'

Excited as she is for the couples' dances, Tess is also looking forward to the group pro numbers. 'Jason Gilkison's choreography is dreamy,' she says. 'Every week he manages to take our breath away. I love the special themed weeks.

'This year, I just can't wait to get going and I'm so grateful to be back. Everyone I've talked to is ready for some light entertainment and sheer *Strictly* glamour. I know I am.'

TEAM PLAYERS

From Halloween horrors to a Disney-themed extravaganza, the group dances are a spectacular showcase of *Strictly*'s professional dancers and take months of planning. Here's how the showstopping pro-dances go from drawing board to dance floor.

With up to 23 routines per series, preparation begins early for Creative Director Jason Gilkison who, together with Executive Producer Sarah James and Series Producer Jack Gledhill, begins gathering ideas and coming up with concepts in June.

'We start by looking at what we did in the last two years – what was most successful, what we really loved,' Jason says.

'We usually have a pie-in-the-sky idea, like a Harry Potter theme or our recent collaboration with Pixar, which might be technically difficult or take a lot of time, so we start making contacts as soon as we can. Then we talk to the accomplished freelance choreographers from all around the UK, or even internationally, and they pitch choreography ideas, telling us what they're seeing on the world stage at the moment.

'We have a giant board around the room that has the launch show, week 1, week 2, Movie Week, Halloween, etcetera, and we put prospective ideas on that. We may have loved the pitch of a choreographer but we need it in a different week, so we go back to them and say, "Do you think you could rework this idea and turn it from Halloween into a Musicals Week number?"

'Over the weeks, we start to see the whole series taking shape on the board, like a jigsaw puzzle, and each year has a different flavour from the one before.'

The next step is to make storyboards for each of the dances, adding ideas for costumes and props, and deciding the potential lead dancers.

'We make sure each pro has a lead in a routine.'

The routines are then approved, and the dance team develop them further, bringing in set designers and adding the music.

'It all feels quite soft at first, just ideas, but once we get the green light we begin to flesh out how to make it incredible,' he says.

'I love seeing how an idea develops into a brilliant dance.'

Jason, who personally choreographs around 17 of the 23 dances each year, begins by coming up with the initial steps and then bouncing ideas off his two assistants. He will then call the pros to find out who is available for the initial 'workshop', where he puts his ideas to the test.

'It can be quite lonely when you're coming up with ideas, so having a couple of dancers to bounce off, plus my two assistants, helps,' he says.

'We get into a studio and start playing the music, seeing which moves sit well on the dancers.'

As Jason will only have the full complement of dancers for one day per number, in rehearsals, he uses this studio time to map out how each pro will move across the floor during the routine.

On a huge table top, which represents the dance floor, he uses named counters, bits of paper and even sweets to represent each pro.

'The biggest difficulty with choreographing group numbers is that you never have those 18 or 20 people in front of you until the rehearsal, and that's when you start to see all the traffic and potential problems.

'We have a big table with little counters where I move around about four "pros" with my hands and someone else moving the other counters that are acting as pros. There are usually four pairs of hands moving them about.'

In August, a few weeks before the launch show, the pros come together for an intensive three-week rehearsal for the group routines. Working at an average of one number per day, the pros perfect between 15 and 17 dances to be performed throughout the series.

'Each dance has to come together within that eight-hour block,' says Jason. 'It sounds like a lot of time, but four hours in the studio is about one minute of TV.

'We're always trying to make it look very fresh and different to what they've done before.'

The secret to success is knowing what you want, but being willing to change your mind, explains Jason.

'The first rule of choreography is that you lock it in and ideally it works exactly how you want it to, but if you see something that could be incredible on the day, that might require 30 seconds of the routine to be completely changed – you want the flexibility to do that.

'When you see the energy of all those pros come into the room, a totally different thing happens. They might react off each other in a completely different way that is far more effective than you realised. It rarely works out exactly as you plan it.'

With limited time, Jason concentrates on the group dances for the first 10 weeks of the run. After Blackpool Week, however, he comes up with fresh numbers using the pro dancers who are no longer in the competition with their partners.

With the majority of the dances under their belt in August, the pros can concentrate on their couple routines.

Amazingly, they need just a quick refresher when it comes to pulling out the group numbers later in the series.

'The pros have each routine filmed on their phones so they can rewatch it and refresh their memory. Then in the week of the actual live show, on the Monday morning, we come on to set for four hours to dust off the dance and add some costumes and props.

'By the end of that Monday morning, we need to be camera ready and then they can go off to work with their celebrity.'

The group get another run-through on Friday morning and, on Saturday, a full dress rehearsal with the live band.

Themed weeks, such as Movie Week and Musicals Week, often have two group dances, which are pre-recorded before and after the main show.

With couples' dances in between, hair and make-up is a huge consideration in the planning.

'Sometimes hair and make-up is very ambitious for the group numbers and the stylists have to work out how the dancers will go from one look to another,' he says.

' For example we really have to consider if somebody in Movie Week is dressed as Shrek and we have to paint them green, ungreen them for the group number, then put them back into green for the results show.

'On Halloween, they might sit in the make-up chair for three hours to get an effect, so if they have spooky make-up for the main show, we will try to keep it for the group number.'

With over 80 group numbers to his name, Jason has a few favourites.

'The launch-show dance for series 16 to Camila Cabello's "Havana" is one which I really loved,' he says. 'I felt we'd actually transported the audience to Havana in the 1950s.

'I also loved the Harry Potter routine in series 16 and the same-sex dance to Imagine Dragons' "Believer". But Blackpool is always great fun, because we try to push it even further with lots of props, lots of effects and extra dancers.

'I feel proud of the group numbers over the last five or six series, because they get more ambitious every year.'

Karen Hauer

Strictly's longest-serving female professional, Karen Hauer, has already competed in eight series and is raring to go with celebrity number nine.

'I can't wait to start working with my celebrity partner,' she says. 'Everybody is so revved up to get onto that dance floor, have a good time and bring happiness to people in their homes. There's so much to look forward to this year in just bringing that *Strictly* sparkle and entertaining people, because we all need a little bit of magic.'

Born in Valencia, Venezuela, Karen took up dancing after moving to New York at the age of eight, winning a scholarship to the Martha Graham School of Contemporary Dance two years later. She studied African, contemporary and ballet dancing before moving on to ballroom and Latin at 19. She was crowned World Mambo Champion in 2008 and Professional American Rhythm Rising Star Champion in 2009.

Karen joined *Strictly Come Dancing* in 2012, reaching week 10 with Westlife's Nicky Byrne. Other partners have included Dave Myers, Jeremy Vine, Charles Venn and Mark Wright, who she took all the way to the Grand Final. Last year, she reached the Semi-final with comedian Chris Ramsey and she says the key to his success was factoring in family time with wife Rosie and their baby son.

'We had a really good understanding of the balance he needed, the amount of hours that were going to go into practice and the time he wanted to be home with his family,' she says. 'That was important, because emotionally and physically it's an intense experience, so we worked it so that he could be at home and still give 100 per cent to *Strictly*. He was brilliant and he responded so well. He wasn't a natural performer in the beginning, but the more he built confidence, the more consistency there was with his performances. He started believing in himself and he had the fans' support because he was so relatable. He had never danced before, so for him to be able to say that he made the Semi-final of *Strictly* is huge.'

As she prepares to meet her next partner, Karen says she is looking for someone who is ready for anything.

'I want a partner who wants to enjoy it, with no stress,' she says. 'I want them to embrace the fulfilment of learning a new skill, but I also want them to have fun. I always want my celebrities to come in with an open mind, because in *Strictly* you can be a Ninja Turtle one day, and Fred Astaire the next!'

In return, Karen wants to reassure them that they are in good hands and she will get the best she can from them.

'I'm very encouraging,' she says. 'I like to push the limits with celebrities, but I want them to feel comfortable and that they can trust me. I like to build their confidence and I want them to enjoy dancing alongside me. But they will sweat a lot! They'll probably have a six-pack by the time I'm done with them, too.'

As a new series dawns, Karen has her eyes firmly on the prize and making it all the way to the Final. 'Two years ago, I made the Quarter-final, last year I made the Semi-final. So let's see what happens this year!'

Katya Jones

Former champ Katya Jones has danced her way to a glitterball trophy with Joe McFadden, partnered Ed Balls in unforgettable routines including the 'Gangnam Style' Salsa and, most recently, earned a rousing ovation for her Quickstep with Mike Bushell.

When it comes to teaching celebrities to dance, as far as Katya is concerned, there's no such word as 'can't'.

'I have what I call aggressive positivity,' she laughs. 'I always say, "Anybody can learn to dance," and I'm there to teach them.

'I never care what sort of dance level they are at or what experience they have had before, or even whether they have rhythm. My job is to teach them to dance and I absolutely love it. I will do everything possible to help them achieve their best.'

The Russian dancer and choreographer believes that the key to a successful partnership is finding a balance.

'It's really important for us to understand the celebrity and their ability. Their personality is so important,' she says. 'They have to be fully committed to dive into the magic world of *Strictly*. The dance has to please the judges technically too, but also never forget that it is an entertainment show and the audience decides. It's a fine balance to perfect, but I love the creativity so much!'

Katya was born in Saint Petersburg and started dancing at the age of six. In 2015, she won the World Professional Latin Showdance Championship and is also the four-time undefeated British National Professional Champion. She joined *Strictly* in series 14, and last year took Mike Bushell to week 8 before also joining him on tour. The BBC sports presenter, she says, was a boundless ball of energy and enthusiasm.

'I don't think either of us had expected to get paired up, but I was very happy because I knew how enthusiastic he was about the whole *Strictly* experience and he was not holding back. On the launch show, he was jumping around and I said, "We're going to put 10 jumps in the first routine. We're going to show them how energetic and enthusiastic you are."

'He worked so hard, and you could clearly see how much fun he was having and the progress he made. We had a wonderful time and we lasted longer than a lot of people predicted – even his family!'

Katya is over the moon to be back on the dance floor for a new series of *Strictly*.

'Everybody is so excited to be together again,' she says. 'We are just so happy to be back, This year, as always *Strictly* is going to be full of fun and glamour, a show the whole family can watch. It's going to be a brilliant series and I can't wait to be dancing and entertaining people again.'

Zoe Ball

This year marks Zoe Ball's tenth series of *It Takes Two* and she can't wait to celebrate with her fellow presenters, *Strictly* dance partner Ian Waite and the whole crew.

'This is my favourite time of year and I absolutely love it,' she says. 'We call it the Return to the Glitter Dome – our little studio of delights. I have worked with the same crew for a decade, but we don't get to see a lot of each other the rest of the year. By summertime we all start messaging each other saying, "It's coming!" I can't wait to see Ian, costume designer Vicky Gill and all the pro dancers. It's like an extended family.'

Sharing presenting duties with Rylan Clark-Neal once again, Zoe has swapped her schedule for this series, fronting the show on Monday to Wednesday, with her co-host taking Thursday and Friday.

'It means I don't get to high-kick down the stairs with him, which is a shame,' she says. 'But we'll see each other on rehearsal days and I'm sure our paths will cross during the course of the series.'

Although he was a newcomer to *It Takes Two* last year, Zoe says her co-presenter was a natural. 'Rylan slotted right in and it was as if he had been there for years,' she says. 'I've always been a bit of a fan girl so to work with him was amazing, and he's such a laugh. He calls me Nana, because I carry this weird little bag around the studio, which has my pens and pencils, my phone, lip balm, throat pastilles and a script. He's always saying, "Don't forget your little Nana bag."

'I love having him on *It Takes Two*, but I would actually like to see him dancing on *Strictly* as a contestant. I can imagine him doing a Cha-cha-cha with those hips. He's done some dancing on the show with the pro dancers and he picks up choreography really quickly, so I think he would be amazing.'

Rylan's dancing prowess aside, Zoe is excited by the new series contestants and can't wait to meet them all. 'I think the line-up is pretty spectacular,' she says. 'When the names came up I was saying, "Yes, Caroline Quentin! Yes, Bill Bailey. Yes, Max George!"

'I'm so happy that Jamie Laing gets to have another go, because everyone was gutted last year when he had an injury and had to drop out. I'm thrilled for Clara Amfo, because I love her and I think she will be a queen. Then there's the excitement of our first all-female pairing, which will be amazing.'

Zoe is also rooting for Bill Bailey, after he used her Radio 2 *Breakfast Show* to reveal he was in the line-up. 'He was hilarious,' she says. 'He told us he was bringing back the hokey-cokey and was calling himself "Caretaker of the Dance", as opposed to the Lord of the Dance. I can't wait to see that famous long hair wafting about the dance floor – and I think he'll rock the Lycra.'

At the start of the series, like many superfans, Zoe likes to guess which celebrities will be paired with which professionals, as well as taking a stab at who will make the Grand Final.

'I always play the guessing game, but last year I only got about three pairings right,' she laughs.'

Born in Blackpool, the home of ballroom, Zoe's love affair with *Strictly* began when she danced her way to the Final in series 3. She took over *It Takes Two* from Claudia Winkleman in 2011.

'I love being part of the *Strictly* family, because you run into former contestants all the time and, once you've done the show, you become part of a little group. It is an endless source of conversation,' she says. 'People talk to me about *Strictly* more than any other thing I've done, especially at this time of year. People of all ages love it, including my family, so it's a joy to be part of such a positive show.'

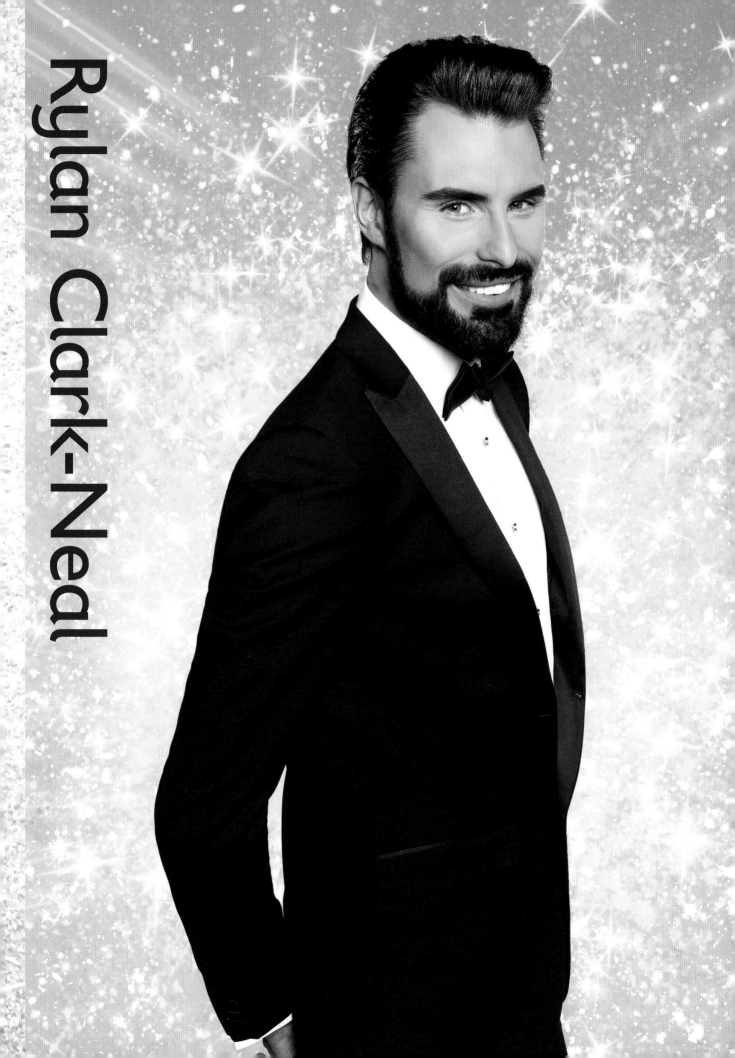

Rylan Clark-Neal

Returning as *It Takes Two* presenter for his second series, Rylan Clark-Neal is looking forward to strutting his stuff on the show.

The Essex-born host kicked off his *It Takes Two* stint last year by dancing a brief Cha-cha-cha with co-host Zoe Ball and says he's learned a lot about ballroom and Latin since coming on board.

'I was taught quite a few dances on the show last year, which was amazing,' he says. 'Everyone was quite shocked because there weren't any major rehearsals for it – I just learned the steps on air and somehow I danced them.

'There is a lot of technical stuff to learn, so, for a novice like me, being thrown in at the deep end of the biggest show on television was eye-opening. But I now know my jetés from my pas de bourrées, shall we say.'

Rylan is a long-time fan of *Strictly Come Dancing* and says *It Takes Two* is the perfect companion show, giving viewers a unique insight into the progress of the contestants.

'You watch the incredible dances on a Saturday night and say, "That was amazing. I wish I could do that,"' he explains. 'But then *It Takes Two* is a proper behind-the-scenes show, so you see the celebrities learning the dance and the progress they make, because they only have a week to learn it. So you see them do some of the steps on Monday and, if they come back on Friday, there's a huge transformation. It shows how hard they've been working.'

Rylan first shot to fame on *The X Factor* and has since presented *Big Brother's Bit on the Side*, *The One Show* and *Ready Steady Cook*. In 2019, he also took over Zoe's Saturday-afternoon slot on Radio 2 but says he is thrilled that *It Takes Two* has given him the opportunity to work alongside her on screen.

'It's been a real pleasure and we get on really well,' he says. 'This year, Zoe is doing Monday to Wednesday and I'm doing Thursday and Friday, but there will be a few crossovers, so we are still very much working alongside each other. I can't wait to catch up with Zoe and see some familiar faces – the camera crew and all the production team, as well as Tess and Claudia, who I love to bits.'

Rylan is also excited about meeting the latest batch of *Strictly* celebrities and welcoming them onto the *It Takes Two* sofa.

'I think the line-up is great this year,' he says. 'It's a really mixed bag of people, so I think there's someone there for everyone. We all know what *Strictly* does, and there might be some people who think, "I'm not too familiar with that person," but then they become your favourite. I'm excited about all of them, so I can't wait to welcome everyone.'

As a newbie last year, Rylan says he 'was welcomed with open arms and had a blast'. Now he's keen to throw himself into another series of *It Takes Two*.

'*Strictly* is loved by everyone and is a real family show,' he says. 'It's the countdown to Christmas and we all deserve a bit of fun and sparkle. It was absolutely amazing to join Team *Strictly* last year – now I'm looking forward to being back in the *Strictly* bubble where life is good.'

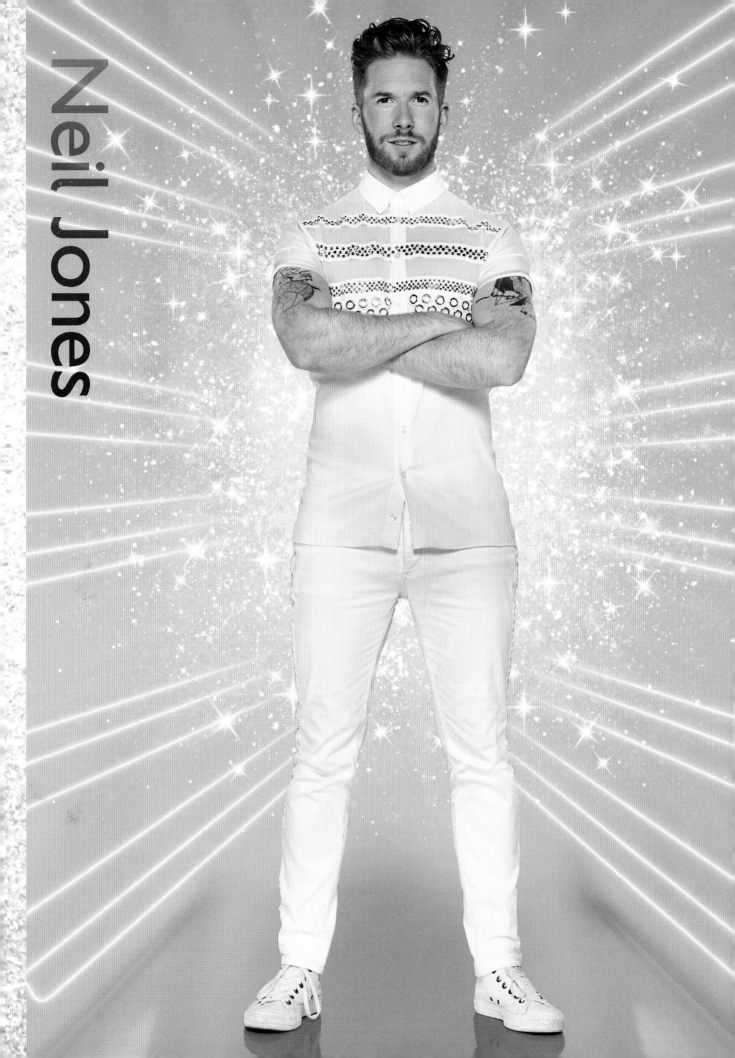

Neil Jones

British dancer Neil Jones is returning for his fifth *Strictly Come Dancing* series and, giving a sneak preview into the spectacular group numbers, he says viewers are in for the best series ever.

'Every year the group routines are incredible, and at the end of the series I always think, "How are they going to top that next year?"' he says. 'But they've hit a high this year. They are some of the best group dances that anyone's ever seen.

'I'm really excited. We have a number called "2020" which is incredible, the set is amazing and the energy is through the roof. There's a truly touching Remembrance Day dance and a brilliant James Bond routine'.

Born in a British army camp in Münster, Germany, Neil started dancing at three and trained in ballet, tap, modern, ballroom and Latin. After teaming up with fellow *Strictly* pro Katya Jones in Blackpool in 2008, they became the undefeated four-time British National Champions, and three-time winners of the World Amateur Latin Championships. He joined the *Strictly* family in 2016 and last year made it to the Quarter-finals with his first celebrity partner, footballer Alex Scott.

'Alex was such a hard worker,' he says. 'I used to wonder how the pros could be in rehearsals for more than seven hours, but Alex and I went well over that, and we didn't even notice the time. At night, when we finished rehearsing, she sent me messages saying, "I've been watching the videos and I'm going to sleep on it tonight. Let me know what I need to improve on." She was a great student.'

Although Neil will not be dancing with a celebrity this year, he is excited to be back on the dance floor. 'As well as the group numbers, I'll be dancing with Nancy Xu during the music acts, so I'm really looking forward to that. Just to be part of *Strictly* is such a great opportunity – I can't wait.'

He is also keen to meet the latest line-up. 'It's a great mix and it works for the whole family,' he says. 'The show is for all different ages and it's important that there's someone there for everybody, then the whole family grows to love them. The great thing is that you can take someone like Joe Sugg, who had a younger fan base, and as he went on the grandparents also fell in love with him. All of this year's celebrities have great personalities, so I can't wait to get to know them.'

The family nature of the show is one of the keys to its lasting success, says Neil.

'The fan base is from young kids all the way up to the grandparents, and they love watching it together,' he says. 'Like a lot of people, when I was growing up Saturday night was family night, when we would sit down together and watch shows like *The Generation Game.* For so long, that's what *Strictly* has been – the programme that brings everybody back together and becomes the topic of conversation. *Strictly* brings positivity, because viewers see the struggles of people learning how to dance and then the success of them actually managing to perform the dance and maybe getting that 10 from the judges. Everybody feels that they're part of that because they're following the contestants and they are with them through every struggle and every celebration.'

Jamie Laing

As a returning celebrity, Jamie Laing has already scored a *Strictly* first. *The Made in Chelsea* star was forced to withdraw from series 17 after sustaining a leg injury, but says he is now fighting fit and ready to pick up where he left off.

'For me, it's one of the shows that we all grew up watching,' he says. 'Honestly, it makes my mum proud that I'm doing it and I've never made her proud before, so that is one of the main reasons I wanted to try again. I came out of it last year and, like most people, I hate failing at stuff, so this is the time to give it another go and go for it.

'If I get injured again it would look like I bottled it, so I really have to be careful, but I'm not worried. I feel pretty fit and healthy.'

Jamie says his biggest supporters are his family, who will be cheering him on all the way – even if they are not convinced of his dancing ability.

'I think my granny was pretty excited and Grandma was over the moon about it,' he says. 'Everyone has been super supportive and everyone I know is really excited. But my mum is obsessed – she can't get enough of it! She is crazy about me being in the show, even though she thinks my dancing is terrible. If I asked her, she would say, "You're awful!" She tells me straight out, "You're not going to win it, there's no way." She reckons I'll be out about week 3!'

Born in Oxford, the reality star and entrepreneur has little dance experience, but thinks his competitive streak could come in useful.

'I want my professional partner to push me to the edge,' he says. 'I'm pretty good at being coached, and I'm pretty competitive. So I need her to push me, make me feel like I've really tried. I don't like losing at anything, especially something I missed out on last year. So I'm going for the win!'

Despite his confidence, Jamie has identified a couple of rivals for the prize.

'I'm freaking out about a few people,' he says. 'I think everyone's looking pretty good. It's going to be a great year.'

If he's worried about the competition on the dance floor, he has no qualms about the costumes.

'Dress me up as a glitterball and give me all the fake tan you can – I can't wait,' he says. 'I want everything. It's going to be unbelievable!'

Bruno Tonioli

Italian judge Bruno Tonioli is starting series 18 with a brand-new look, and his silver-fox hair has already caused quite a stir. But he is delighted with the positive reaction he's been getting from *Strictly* fans.

'I can't believe it,' he says. 'I decided it was time for a change, time to reinvent myself. It was a big change, because when you've been doing what I do for such a long time people tend to identify you as that persona. But this has been empowering in a way, because the reaction has been fantastic, so I'm very pleased.'

The effusive judge is bouncing with excitement over the 2020 recruits and is expecting a few surprises when the couples present their first few dances.

'The line-up is fantastic,' he says. 'The great thing about the show is that whatever you think at the beginning, it always surprises you, because suddenly the Stacey Dooleys and Kelvin Fletchers come out, and you think, "Wow!" That's why the show is so strong and people like it, because you can never predict how it's going to play out. Out of the blue, people become dancers and that gets people hooked.

'This year there is a great mix, and they all look good on paper. Caroline Quentin is an amazing actress – funny, with a great personality – and Bill Bailey is a great comedian. They all have qualities to make this a very interesting show, but until you see them dancing a couple of times it is impossible to tell. Then we have two girls dancing together, which is fantastic and was entirely Nicola Adams's choice, so good for her. There will be a lot of eyes on them, but, at the same time, she will be judged exactly like everyone else.'

Bruno can't wait to see his fellow judges this year. 'I am looking forward to the laughs with the other judges, and Claudia and Tess. It is like your family, when you leave home. You've been together for such a long time and you're always going to be attached to your family, forever. That's never going to change.'

Bruno's advice to the incoming contestants is that there's no substitute for hard work. 'You've got to put the time in,' he says. 'You're not going to get a high score just by turning up! The contestants need to apply themselves and listen to their professionals, learn from them. It's no secret that it really pays off to work at it.'

For tips on how to reach the Final, the contestants and pros should take a leaf out of Kelvin Fletcher and Oti Mabuse's book.

'Last year's Final was fantastic and incredibly close,' he says. 'It was so unpredictable because they were all so good, but it really shows how you have to play it. It is about choices that the public will connect to, because at that stage we judges have said our thing and they all deserve to win. Kelvin and Oti really got it with their showdance.'

HRVY

As a singer, HRVY reckons he can bust a move or two, but he's looking forward to learning a new skill, in ballroom and Latin – and he's aiming for glitterball glory.

'I've always loved dancing and I would say I can move my hips a bit,' he says. 'I just love the idea of the challenge, and I'm so competitive. I really want to win it, 100 per cent. Obviously it's the taking part that counts, but I think everyone wants to go for gold! I'm going to put my heart into it, and that's why I want to win it.'

Born in Kent, HRVY released his first single, 'Thank You', in 2013 at the age of 14. A year later he supported Little Mix on tour and landed a job as a presenter on CBBC show *Friday Download.* Now his stint on *Strictly* has given his family something else to be excited about.

'My nan is buzzing,' he says. 'She left me countless voicemails just saying how excited she is. She'll ring me up every day and tell me what's in the news. She's always watched the show and she's a big fan, so this is going to be a big, proud moment to watch me on TV every week. She's going to love it!

'My mum's received loads of texts from all of her friends, and I've seen social-media statuses from my old school teachers, so it's been a really positive reaction and it's made me a lot more excited.'

The up-and-coming popstar, who has over 10 million followers on social media, says the reaction from his friends has also been 'pretty mad'.

'Obviously I knew it was huge, the biggest show in the UK, but I just didn't realise how many of my friends, especially younger friends, watch the show. They think it's amazing. I didn't realise how much of a broad audience *Strictly* has.'

Although he's keen to meet all his fellow celebrities, HRVY admits he has a special reason for wanting to hang out with Max George.

'Weirdly, I went to The Wanted's last concert when I was younger,' he says. 'When I was backstage I was like, "Oh my God, there's Max and everyone else!" He won't remember me, but I was a big fan so that's really cool. I think it's nice that there's such a mix of different people. When I saw the line-up, I was really happy and they all seem like lovely people.'

Saffron Barker, who competed in series 17, is a friend and has already dished out some advice to her fellow influencer. 'She said that I'm going to love it,' he reveals. 'She told me that I have to work hard, obviously, but enjoy it. She was so jealous that I was doing it because she wished she could go back and do it all again!'

Although he's never danced ballroom and Latin before, HRVY thinks the slower dances will be the toughest for him. 'I am into the quicker, up-tempo, energetic dancing, but I'm quite excited to do ballroom,' he says. 'I feel the more composed dances can be harder, because sometimes the slower the dance, the more technical and precise you need to be, because it's easier for the eye to see mistakes. They might be harder than the quick dances and I really want to give myself a challenge and do more of the ballroom.'

As well as the challenge of dancing, HRVY is game for a touch of glamour. 'I might stay away from the fake tan, but apparently all the boys say that and then by week 4 they are like, "I think I might need to be a bit more bronze." But I don't mind – put me in anything. I'm there for all the diamonds and dazzle!'

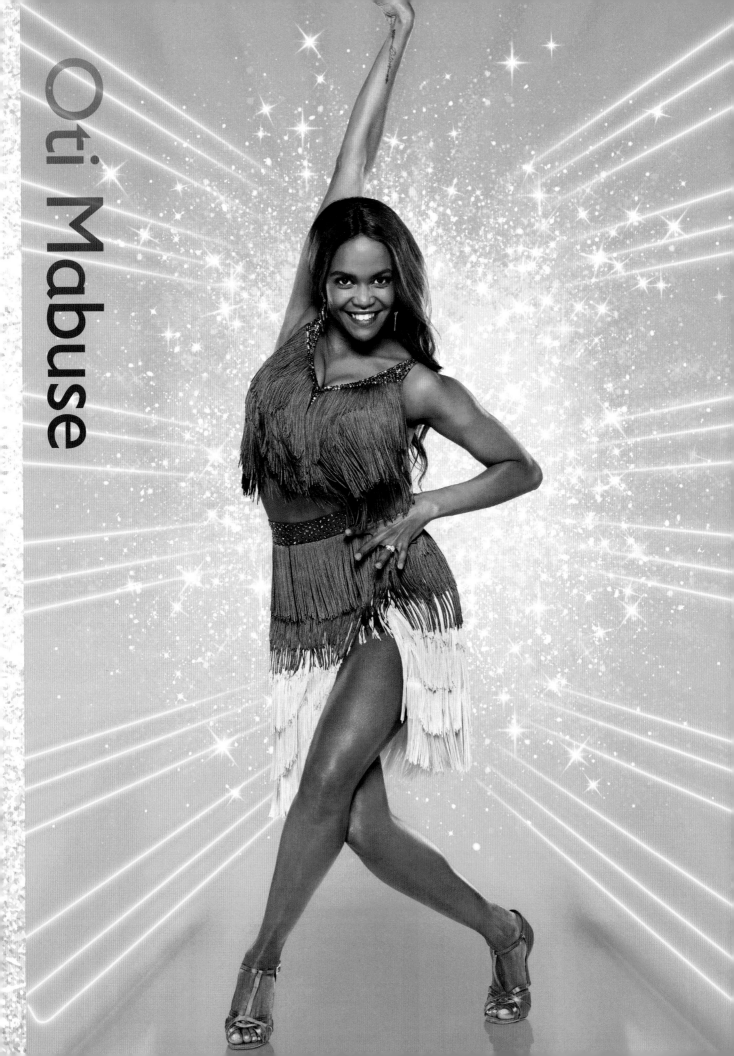

Oti Mabuse

Current *Strictly* champ Oti Mabuse lifted the glitterball in 2019 with Kelvin Fletcher in a thrill-packed Final that saw the couple pick up a perfect score for their whirlwind showdance.

'I still get goosebumps talking about it,' says Oti. 'It was an unbelievable dream come true. I still remember everything about it – the lights, the props, the feeling that you get just before you go on and how excited we were after we nailed the dance. My husband and my godmother were in the audience and I had a lot of support from the public. It was an unbelievable night.'

As a pupil, Oti says Kelvin was diligent and disciplined, sharing many of her own qualities.

'Kelvin is hard-working, very detail-orientated and a perfectionist, which could be describing myself,' she says. 'We were two competitive perfectionists and we literally became obsessed with the dances. That's all we talked about and all we wanted to do. We surrounded ourselves with it and it made sense that he did so well.'

Born in Pretoria, South Africa, Oti began dancing as a young child, following in the footsteps of older sister Motsi, who is also a professional dancer and now a *Strictly* judge. She studied civil engineering at university, but dancing was her true passion and, after gaining her degree, she moved to Germany to compete. Oti is the eight-time South African Latin American champion and has also claimed an array of titles, including World European Latin semi-finalist and World Cup Championship semi-finalist.

Oti joined *Strictly* in 2015, reaching the Final a year later with actor Danny Mac, where they were pipped to the post by Ore Oduba and Joanne Clifton. Since then she has partnered Paralympian Jonnie Peacock and cricketer Graeme Swann before finally romping to victory last year.

The win came after a disappointing start, when Oti's original partner, Jamie Laing, had to drop out due to injury. 'I was sad about Jamie because he is a unique and special type of human being,' she says. 'He's fun, he's young, he is charming and charismatic, and I was looking forward to seeing how far I could teach him. So, obviously, it was a blow, but then Kelvin came along and changed the narrative of that series, so I'm so grateful I could still compete and I'm also thrilled that Jamie is back this year as the comeback kid.'

Having tasted glory, Oti says she expects similar commitment from her celebrity partner this year.

'My celebrity should come with the attitude to work hard,' she says. 'I'm now coming from a place of experience, now I know what it took to win last year. I want them to come into the show and have no inhibitions. I just want them to embrace everything that they get hit with.'

Oti is excited by the line-up this year and looking forward to meeting them all.

'I think they're amazing,' she says. 'I've been a huge fan of Clara Amfo for years, so I'm thrilled she's on the show. HRVY has a massive following but it's not about who you are, it's about what you deliver on the show. We have a popstar in Max George and I hear Caroline Quentin is very funny and is likely to surprise us. The whole line-up is very exciting and it's great because, as a pro, you don't only make friends with your own celebrity but with all the others, too.'

Before they go into the rehearsal room, Oti has one simple piece of advice for the new recruits. 'My advice to them would just be trust your pro,' she says. 'This is the most important connection that you will have with anyone in the next few weeks, so create a team with your mentor and listen to them.'

Claudia Winkleman

As she gears up for the new series of *Strictly Come Dancing*, Claudia Winkleman is excited about the line-up. While the latest celebrities to take on the challenge cover all ages and walks of life, Claudia says they will all have each other's backs throughout the competition.

'The line-up is absolutely stupendous,' she says. 'I screamed out loud when the producer told us who was on board. I love Clara Amfo, Caroline Quentin and Maisie Smith, and I think they're all fantastic.

'They're going to fit together superbly. The great thing about *Strictly* is that the only other people who understand what they're going through are the others in that cohort, so they always end up really looking after each other. I saw 2016 contestant Ed Balls recently and he told me the group from his year still stay in touch. That's what I hear from many contestants and I love that about the show.'

Claudia, who has co-presented the live show with Tess Daly since 2014, is reluctant to speculate on the potential of the new *Strictly* stars but says she is looking forward to watching them all progress.

'I know nothing about their dancing ability at this stage, so I don't know who's going to shine on the dance floor,' she says. 'But I can't wait to see them all and I think they're fantastic for doing it. I'm pleased to see Jamie Laing back, because he is so charming and funny. The poor boy was so excited to take part [last year] and then, of course, he couldn't, and he saw his stand-in, Kelvin Fletcher, go on to win. So this year he is going to come back feeling all the more competitive.

'I'm absolutely over the moon that we have our first same-sex couple as well, and I think Nicola Adams will be great. Sports stars and Olympians know what it takes to train, and they always put the hours in, which really helps.'

While Claudia loves all the amazing costumes on the show, there is one contestant she is eager to see in sparkly spandex as he struts his stuff in the studio. 'Bill Bailey is hilarious,' she says. 'For me, he has to do very little. Just to see him in the Latin dance get-up will be enough. But I think they'll all be fantastic and hugely entertaining.'

After eight months away from the show, Claudia is keen to be reunited with co-presenter Tess, the backstage crew and the judges.

'Motsi made a wonderful debut last year,' says Claudia. 'She's so charming and funny and I think she's absolutely faultless, so I'm very pleased she's back. I can't wait to see Shirley, our head judge, and Craig and Bruno too. They are all great.

She is also looking forward to seeing the professional dancers and watching them take to the floor.

'The professional dancers are the heartbeat of the show,' she says. 'When I come on to that dance floor and they are all dancing in unison, I still get full-body goosebumps. They light up the whole show, so I can't wait to see them and watch the fabulous group dances.'

Janette Manrara

American-born Janette Manrara is one of the longest-serving pros on the show, with seven years under her belt. But this year she wants to get further in the competition than she has ever done before.

'I'm looking forward to doing what I love to do the most, which is dance,' she says. 'And hopefully, fingers crossed, this year I will get to the Final! That would be amazing. I can't wait to start teaching a celebrity, creating routines, dancing with my new partner and putting it all together. I want to enjoy dancing with somebody who is willing to grow and learn along with me.'

Growing up in Florida, Janette began dancing at musical-theatre school at 12, although she was a latecomer to professional dancing. She studied finance at the University of Florida and worked in a bank for seven years, while training in her spare time in jazz, ballet, pointe, flamenco, hip-hop and ballroom.

She joined *Strictly* in 2013 and has danced with Julien Macdonald, Peter Andre, Melvin Odoom, Aston Merrygold and Dr Ranj Singh, as well as reaching the Semi-final with Jake Wood in 2014. Last year, she partnered Paralympian Will Bayley, who had to leave the competition in week 6 due to injury, but Janette says he was the model pupil.

'Will was one of the best,' she says. 'He worked so hard. He was an absolute dream of a student and every week he would surprise me. We accomplished and created such a lot in that room together, so I really felt like it was a journey that we shared together. I loved dancing with him. It was a wonderful year.'

One dance, their week-5 Couple's Choice to Lukas Graham's '7 Years', was a particular highlight for both performers. 'I'm so happy that we were able to do our Contemporary number, because that was the one that I wanted to accomplish, to tell Will's inspirational story. He's such an incredible human being, and to be able to share that through dancing and music was one of the most special things I've ever done on *Strictly*. Although we had to end our *Strictly* journey earlier than we hoped, Will is doing really well now and we created a moment that I know I'm going to cherish in my heart forever.'

Moving forward, Janette has been getting to know the new contestants – even before she meets them.

'I like to do some online research on the celebrities, like just watching a few things they've posted and try to get to know their personalities a little via the internet.' she says. 'They all seem absolutely lovely. I have met Max George before and I'm a big fan of Caroline Quentin, because of the TV shows I've watched her in, but I was just excited to get to know them all.'

From her own partner, Janette is expecting fun – and a lot of hard work. 'I want to be with somebody who is willing to work really hard but is also coming in with joy in their heart to be part of the show and performing every Saturday night.

'I'm feeling really creative, and that means I come up with many different ways of doing things. Whoever I get is going on a creative ride with me – and a hyper ride, because I have loads of energy.'

But Janette promises she won't be too hard on her new recruit.

'As a teacher, I'm tough when I need to be tough, but I never forget this is an entertainment show,' she says. 'I want to make myself, my partner and everybody else at home happy.'

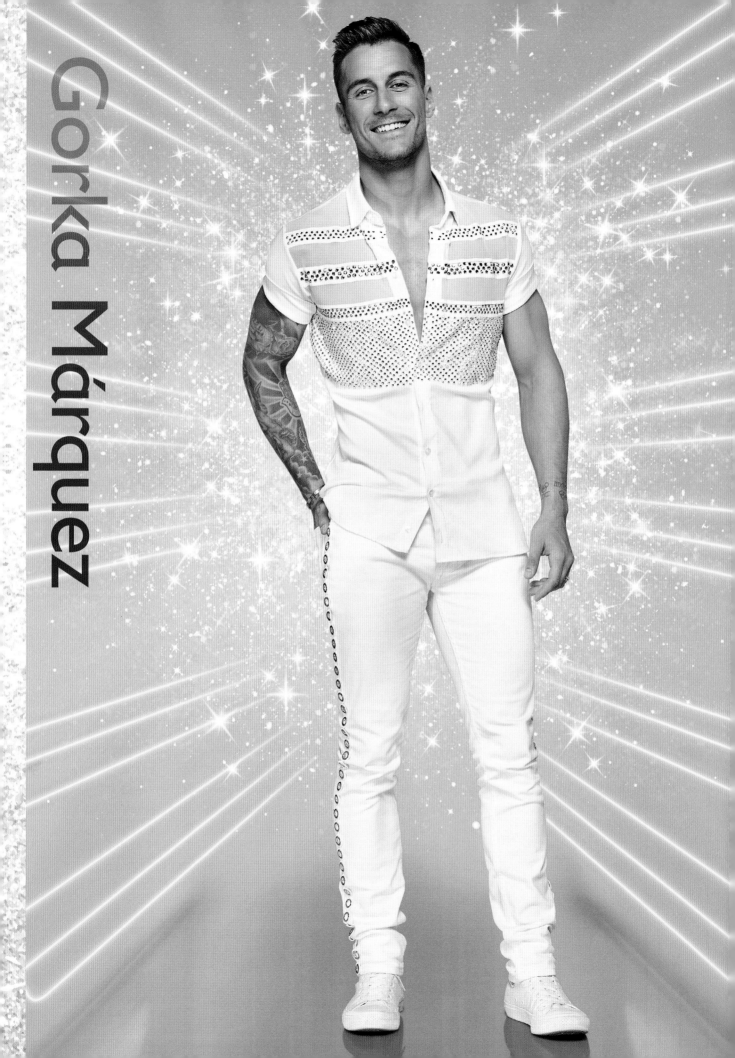

Gorka Márquez

Former finalist Gorka Márquez is going into his fifth year on *Strictly* and he promises viewers are in for a treat from the professional routines, as well as the couples' dances.

'This year's group dances are epic!' he says. 'I have been five years in the show and I can tell you that this year we are raising the bar. I love all of them. They are so different but so good, and every aspect of the production – choreography, costumes, music, lighting, props and all the pros – is just amazing.'

Having begun to dance at the age of 11, Gorka soon became one of the top dancers in his native Spain, representing his country in the World Latin Championships in 2010 and reaching the semi-finals of the 2012 WDSF World Cup. He then joined the *Strictly* family in 2016 partnering *EastEnders* star Tameka Empson. The following year he made the Final with Alexandra Burke, narrowly missing out to Joe McFadden and Katya Jones, and in 2018 he was paired with TV presenter and charity campaigner Katie Piper, bowing out in week 4.

Although he wasn't partnered with a celebrity in series 17, Gorka made a very special appearance on the Christmas special, dancing the Jive with partner Gemma Atkinson and introducing the couple's baby, Mia – then five months old – to viewers.

'Last year was an amazing year,' he says. 'It was different as I didn't take part in the competition, but I loved being part of the show. It gave me a chance to see it all from a different perspective and see how much work everyone puts into it, and also to enjoy the amazing numbers from all the couples. I really loved it.'

This year, he has plenty of ideas for routines and can't wait to get into the rehearsal room. 'I'm really looking forward to getting to know my partner for this series,' he says. 'I can't wait to start creating amazing numbers, to tell stories and convey emotions through dance and to be able to teach someone and see her grow and learn.'

In the months leading up to the series, Gorka has been preparing by working out but has also been improving his teaching skills.

'I think dance is a fantastic way to keep fit and enjoy it, without feeling you're working out,' he says.

Back in the dance studio, Gorka is energised for another fabulous series of *Strictly*.

'I think it's going to be amazing this year,' he says. 'One of the best things about the show, and one of the reasons it is so successful, is that it makes everyone happy. It is a show full of joy, love and passion. Everyone who works on the show, from the production crew and dancers to make-up and costume, loves the show. You can feel that as a spectator, and it is uplifting.'

LIGHTS, CAMERA, ACTION!

Broadcast live every Saturday night, *Strictly Come Dancing* allows viewers to enjoy every moment as if they were sitting at the side of the dance floor.

On the other side of the lens, bringing that studio experience into your living room, is a talented team of camera operators, whose precision and accuracy ensure that the live shows run smoothly time after time.

Here, we go behind the cameras to meet the crew. Beyond the dance floor and audience seating area, the George Lucas studio at Elstree is a mass of cables for cameras, lights and sound equipment.

Each dance routine is captured by ten cameras, including four fixed-pedestal cameras, three hand-held cameras on long cables, a wireless hand-held Steadicam and a techno crane – a huge telescopic arm that reaches out across the dance floor to get shots from above.

Before the Friday rehearsal, each operator is sent a camera script, which tells them which camera is needed for each shot.

The crucial task of mapping that out falls to Series Director Nikki Parsons.

'As soon as the dancers are happy with their routine, usually on Tuesday or Wednesday, they send me a recording in a locked-off wide shot,' she reveals.

'The music is then broken down into bars and beats by the script supervisor, then I mark on my tablet when to cut, which camera is taking each shot, a shot description and how long that shot should be.

'That all goes into a scripted breakdown, with numbered shots, which is sent to other departments so that everyone can make sure they're in the right place at the right time.'

The camera cuts can be dictated by the pace of the dance, as well as the style.

'I approach them all differently,' explains Nikki. 'I've learned over the years what works best in each kind of genre because some dances, like the Salsa, tend to face the front, without moving round the floor, so you have a faster cut pace to bring it to life, whereas something like a Waltz can be so beautiful, demanding longer, more lingering shots.'

Nikki also has to take into account props that need to be moved or taken off the floor during a routine, and special effects, as well as the couples' entrance.

'We might have a gate in the middle of the dance floor at the beginning of a routine, then, while we home in on the dancers, the stage crew are behind the camera taking it away.

'They take their cue from the camera script, so if someone has thrown a cane onto the floor and it needs to be removed, I can tell them, "On shot 12, go onto the floor and pick it up," because at that point we are shooting in the other direction.

'If there's a special effect, such as a firework happening a third of the way through, we'll note down, "Shot 22, pyro." Then, at shot 22, on a cue from me, the special-effects team will fire the pyro.

'It's complicated to work out and it just looks like a lot of numbers and words, but the camera script is crucial.'

On Thursday afternoon Nikki and Executive Producer Sarah James meet with the dance team, Series Producers, Lighting Director, Set Designer and all the heads of department to talk through the performances for the coming week and the week after.

The camera scripts are then sent out to Camera Supervisor Lincoln Abraham, Steadicam Operator Dominic Jackson and all the camera crew ahead of Friday rehearsal, when each couple brings their routine to the studio for the first time.

'Each couple has a 20-minute rehearsal on a Friday, which gives us a good idea of how we want the dance to look,' says Nikki.

'Then we can make changes if something doesn't work, but they are only small tweaks, perhaps to the props, the lighting, the graphics or camera shots.'

While Nikki is working towards Saturday night

most of the week, the job for Lincoln and his team begins on Friday morning.

'Nikki makes our job so much easier because she knows how she wants it to look,' he says. 'She's an ex-dancer and has it all scripted down to the beats and the bars by the time we come in.

'Every camera has a shot card, on our tablets, which tells us which shot is required at which time.

'If something can't be done, we'll discuss alternatives and work out how to achieve what Nikki wants so she always gets a result.'

As Steadicam operator, Dominic is the most mobile of the camera crew and his job is to run around the outside of the dance floor to get shots from every angle. During Friday rehearsals his assistant – known as a focus puller, because they adjust the focus on the camera – makes copious notes to add to the cards.'We have a script supervisor who counts the musical bars and calls the shots,' he says. 'But because I am moving about the studio, I spend a lot of time making sure I'm not going to be in the previous shot, so a lot of prep goes into staying out of the way.'

On Saturday, the camera crew are back for dress rehearsals, where the live band and the full costumes are introduced for the first time.

Nikki spends much of the day in the gallery, the production hub at the back of the main studio, directing the show through the talkback system, which allows her to speak to crew in the main studio.

'The heads of department have their own teams, but I'm the key communication point in the studio for lighting, sound, the floor team, the cameras, etcetera,' she says. 'So everything is fed through me, and the team in the gallery and I direct the cameras and make sure we're getting the right shots and that the dances look their best.

'Hopefully by the time it goes to the live show, it's all worked out and I only have to give the odd cue.'

As well as leading the camera team, Lincoln is behind camera one, which is mounted on a pedestal but can move about and spin in a 360-degree circle.

'When the couples come down the stairs at the start of the show, my camera is on the dance floor because the lenses are not long enough to get those shots,' he explains.'Then we go to a VT and we come off the dance floor. After that, the only camera on the floor will be the Steadicam, which has no cable, and Dominic may also be on the balcony if the dance starts there.'

Saturday is an action-packed day for Dominic, who spends much of it sprinting around the studio with a 28kg camera strapped to his chest.

'I am on my feet during dance routines, but the camera has a stand and I get to rest during the VT,' he says.

'I have worn a step counter on occasion, and I average between 17,000 and 22,000 steps on a *Strictly* Saturday, so it's quite hard on your feet.

'I average between 17,000 and 22,000 steps on a *Strictly* Saturday'

'Over the years, I've found one particular make of trainers that give me the support I need, because sometimes, when I'm running in circles around the dance floor, often side on to the camera, I'm leaning to keep the camera upright so I'm literally running on the edges of my trainers.

'I'm very fussy about my footwear, and when we go on a break I put on a pair of driving slippers so my trainers aren't worn outside.'

The dance floor is swept between each routine, to make sure a stray bead or sequin can't cause the dancers or cameramen to slip, and Dominic is careful that no water is spilt.

'When the dancers have new shoes, they sometimes wet and scrape the sole of the shoe, to give them more grip,' he says.

'The dancers now have a little bit of carpet off set where they can wet their shoes, which ensures the dance floor is kept dry.'

The Steadicam is counterbalanced by a weight underneath the camera, on a post, and it is mounted on a highly sprung metal arm attached to a custom-made vest, which absorbs the operator's movement.

But Dominic, who has worked on the show since series one, says cameras have got a lot lighter and technology has moved on leaps and bounds.

'When we first started, I was lucky if a battery

lasted a whole routine,' he says. 'As soon as I put the camera down, I had to change it. Now they last for 45 minutes, are much smaller and power everything.' Because I'm wireless, whereas the other cameras are plugged into the mains, the last thing I need to be worried about is whether the battery is going to go flat halfway through a routine.

'Some things have got lighter, too. I can now put a light on the rig, which the lighting department can control wirelessly, as well as controlling the colour temperature and how bright it is.

'The lens has also got a bit wider, which means if I'm doing a 360, I don't have to run in such a big circle, which makes my life a little bit easier.'

Most of the crew return year after year, and for Lincoln, that means peace of mind.

'We have a pool of people that have worked on the show and know how it works,' he says.

'That means I don't need to worry about anybody, because everybody excels at what they do.

'I have an absolutely fantastic team and it's a pleasure to work with them. It's like a family and we have a laugh, but when game time comes we all switch on.

'With a live show going out to millions, there's always pressure, but it's a good pressure, because everybody works as a team and we help each other out, so we get a great show at the end of the day.'

With no commercial breaks, the crew have just 90 seconds between dances to reset the scene and move scenery for the next couple, which means running on a tight schedule. 'If something goes wrong you have to fight the flames, but usually the live show is a well-run ship that sails calmly through the waters,' says Nikki.

'Everyone works at the top of their game when it's a live show. The challenge is to make it seamless and easy to watch, so viewers can enjoy *Strictly* and not even think about all the hard work that goes on behind the scenes.'

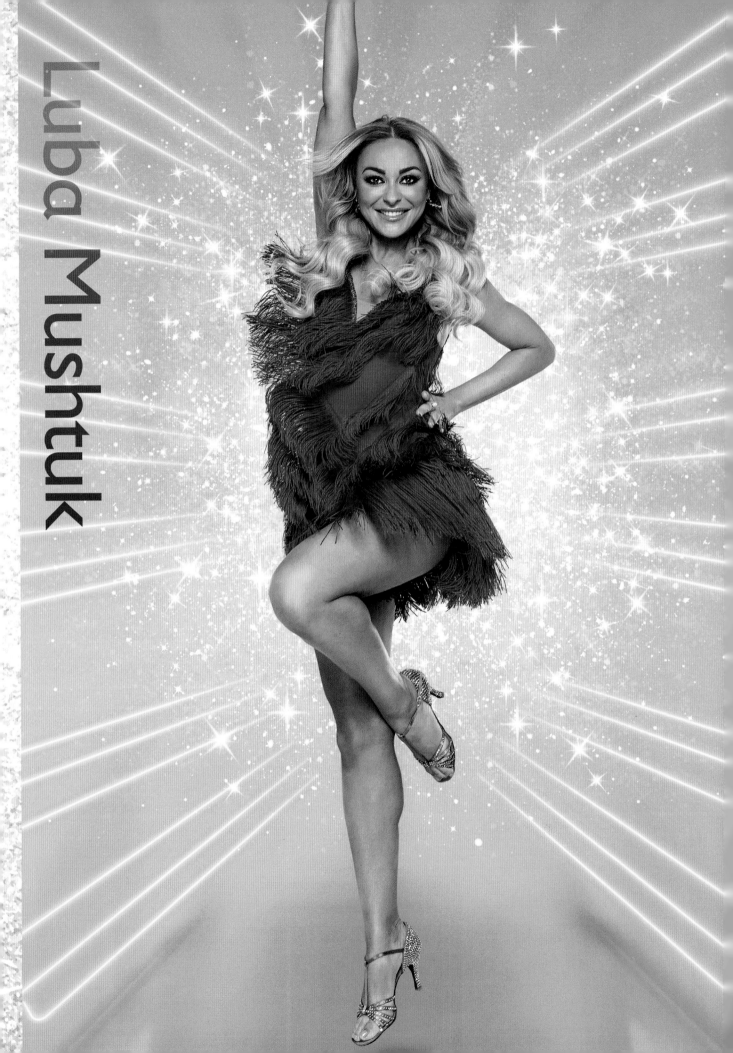

Luba Mushtuk

Back for a second year in the Strictly spotlight, Luba Mushtuk is keen to add a little magic to everyone's Saturday night.

'I'm looking forward to bringing some joy and happiness through the screen to all the people watching us on Saturday night,' she says. 'I hope we can help bring some warmth and sparkle into people's homes and transport them to the wonderful, glittering, gorgeous world of Strictly!'

The Russian-born dancer and choreographer is coming into this series well prepared, having spent the summer looking for inspiration for her fabulous routines.

'We are always trying to be creative because we never want to do the same thing, from year to year,' she says. 'We want to surprise the audience with a different lift or a different way of doing the same dances, by putting a different spin on them. So I used this break to think, plan and inspire myself with movies and dance shows.'

Luba is four-time winner of the Italian Dance Championship, and Italian Open Latin Show Dance champion. Although she's been part of the Strictly family for many years as assistant choreographer, she joined the professional dancers in 2018 and, last year, was paired with Olympic rower James Cracknell.

'James is a sweetheart and it was just amazing to start that journey with him,' she says. 'I will never forget that series because he was my first official celebrity partner and it was great to teach him.'

Even though they were first to leave the competition, James came on leaps and bounds under Luba's expert tutelage.

'At the start he said, "I've never danced in my life. I have two left feet and two left arms,"' says Luba. 'My job was to build his confidence and tell him, "You actually can [dance]." By the time we did the Jive in week two, he was enjoying it so much he said, "This is the best thing ever."'

As a teacher, Luba believes that anyone can learn to dance, with time and effort. 'It's not only dancing; that's how I approach life,' she says. 'Nothing falls from the sky, so you need to work for everything. With dance, some people have it more naturally and some have to work a bit harder, because they have a different feel for the music or a different body, but anyone can dance. I will always say it and Strictly celebrities always prove it.'

The talented professional is also a passionate advocate of dance as a fun form of regular exercise – for both body and mind.

'I truly believe dancing is not only about getting fit physically,' she says. 'It's training for both your body and your brain, and it's so good for everyone.'

Giovanni Pernice

With a hat-trick of appearances in the Grand Final, Giovanni Pernice is going for the glitterball this year. So he is planning to hit the ground running with his celebrity partner.

'I want somebody to work hard because I'm very competitive,' he says. 'Obviously, you want to have a good time in the studio with no drama, and so far I've been so lucky with my partners. But I want them to enjoy our time together and, obviously, put in the hours and put some magic on that floor.'

For his celebrity, he has one piece of valuable advice. 'Listen to me,' he says simply. 'Trust me, because at the end of the day, we pros want to train our partners to be good dancers and have a good time together.'

Born in Sicily, Giovanni took up dance lessons at a young age and left home at 14 to study at a world-class dance school in Bologna. He began competing as an adult in 2008, and in 2012 he was crowned the Italian champion. He has also competed in numerous international dance competitions all over the world. He joined *Strictly* in 2015, reaching the Grand Final with *Coronation Street* actress Georgia May Foote and scoring a perfect 40 for their incredible Charleston. He made it to the Grand Final once again in 2017, with Debbie McGee, and the following year with

Faye Tozer. Last year, he was partnered with Michelle Visage and made it to Blackpool and week 9 before being eliminated.

'Michelle and I are both strong personalities, but we became very good friends,' he says. 'You spend so much time in the room together so by the end of the series, I know exactly how my celebrity works and she knows exactly how I work. I loved our Halloween Foxtrot, to *The Addams Family* theme. And getting 39 from the judges is always a bonus!'

When it comes to the comments from the judges, Giovanni is philosophical about any feedback the couple might get.

'Everybody has a different opinion, so one person might like a dance and another won't,' he says. 'The judges all have minds of their own, but you need to accept everything that they say because they know what they're talking about. So we have to take the comments on board and try to make it better.'

In preparation for the new series, the Sicilian dancer has been thinking about new routines and is excited about meeting his celebrity partner. 'I always find some inspiration, from videos and other sources, but until I know who my partner is I can't really start to come up with the routines because I might think of some choreography for one person, but then it won't work for my partner.

'But I am really looking forward to going into the studio and spending hours teaching my partner to dance and getting to know them. I can't wait.'

Gethin Jones

Former *Strictly* contestant Gethin Jones has been the backstage eyes and ears on *It Takes Two* since 2016, bringing viewers a weekly update from Elstree.

Every Friday, he goes behind the scenes at the studio rehearsal to chat to the celebrities and pros and get a sneak peek at the treats in store on Saturday night.

The Welsh presenter, who reached the Semi-final with Camilla Dallerup in series 5, says the job is perfect for him because Friday was always his favourite day in the competition. 'Saturday was amazing, but it would pass in a bit of a blur,' he says. 'But on Friday you get to see the other people you're competing against and hang out. There's a break before the practice run of the eliminations when everyone is together, and there's always lots of chat.

'Being there on a Friday for *ITT* is a real privilege and it reminds me of when I did the show myself. Watching the guys rehearse is fascinating, because it's never the same studio as they've rehearsed in and they've been dancing to a track, not the live music of the band.

'It's like one big family, because I've known some of the pros for 12 years, so it's great to hang out there.

'Friday is a mixture of busy and relaxed. You can feel that something's coming and the celebrities know that in the next 24 hours they could be leaving the competition. So there's an element of focus as well.'

Although he occasionally watches the live show in the studio, on most Saturday nights he is glued to his TV at home.

'I'm usually chatting to my sister and my mum in the family WhatsApp group, discussing each dance like any fan. I love watching it on Saturday and comparing it to what I saw on Friday – what they did differently in rehearsals. I'm a bit of a geek when it comes to *Strictly*!'

Gethin, who started his career on Welsh-language children's shows before becoming a *Blue Peter* presenter in 2005, reveals that it was Zoe Ball who first suggested he should take a turn on the *Strictly* floor.

'I went to watch the 2005 Semi-final with my fellow *Blue Peter* presenter Liz Barker, and Zoe was competing,' he recalls.

'As she walked offstage I was clapping enthusiastically, and she caught my eye and mouthed, "You should do this next year." I remember thinking at the time, "Absolutely no way. This is completely out of my comfort zone." Six months later, I was building a shelter in a Bolivian jungle [for a *Blue Peter* special] and I got a phone call saying, "Do you want to do *Strictly*?" I thought, "It can't be harder than this," so I said, "Okay, fine." I had completely forgotten the fear I felt when I watched it.'

It's certainly not a decision he regrets – and his family couldn't have been happier.

'It was the best three months of my life,' he says. 'My sister and my mum are massive fans, so they were over the moon. My little nephew Albie was a baby and my sister Mererid brought him up for every show. She would watch the first half of the show and then swap over when he needed feeding and Dad would watch the rest of it.

'Every week she dressed Albie in the sequins I was wearing, and at the end of it she made a book out of the pictures.'

Despite insisting that he 'couldn't dance for toffee' before partnering Camilla, Gethin danced his way to the Semi-final and bagged an impressive 37 points for his Jive.

'That was entirely down to Camilla,' he says. 'I've always said it is the pros that make the show, because they take someone who's not the best dancer to start with and turn them into one, which is incredible. In the same way, they take someone who does have rhythm and dance ability and push them to another level. That's a tremendous skill.'

Cardiff-born Gethin came back into the *Strictly* fold in 2015, presenting *Dancing with the Stars'* sister show, *All Access*, in the US. A year later he became the roving reporter on *It Takes Two*.

Being on set means he gets a close look at all the fabulous routines, and occasionally he even wishes he were on the floor himself.

'In my head I can still dance like a mixture of Giovanni, Gorka and Aljaž,' he says. 'But the reality is, I'm probably a little bit more like Ed Balls doing "Gangnam Style"!'

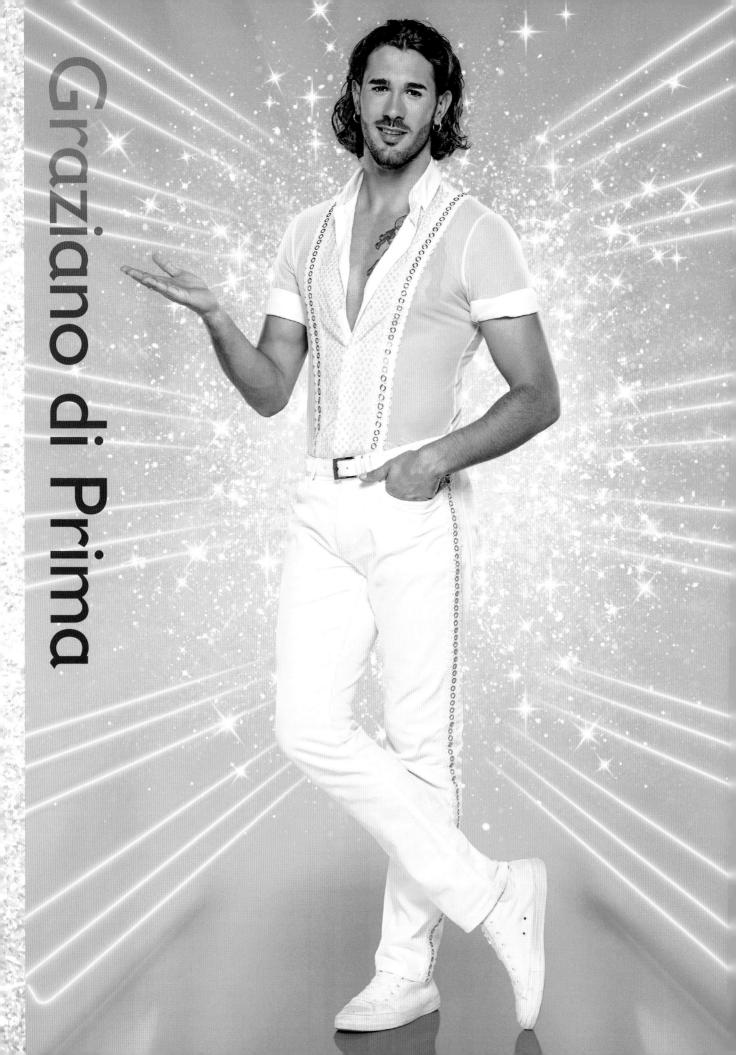

Graziano di Prima

On his third outing on *Strictly Come Dancing*, Graziano di Prima is over the moon to be back in the fold and says he is anticipating another brilliant series.

'I'm so excited,' he says. 'I can't wait to meet the new bunch of celebrities and, like every season, to try and bring the energy as much as I can. I'm really looking forward to it. When the professional dancers first started rehearsals and were back together again, we were crying with happiness. Being part of this amazing *Strictly* family is everything to me!'

Born in Sicily, Graziano is an Italian Latin Champion, who has also represented Belgium at the World Championships. He joined *Strictly* in 2018, dancing with DJ Vick Hope. Last year, he was paired with *Holby City* actress Chizzy Akudolu for the Christmas special, dancing a Cha-cha-cha. He also made it into the *Guinness World Records* for the most Botafogo dance steps in 30 seconds, with 90 steps, breaking former *Strictly* pro Artem Chigvintsev's record of 79. But the personal highlight of the series was dancing with Johannes Radebe in the show's first same-sex professional dance, during Emeli Sandé's performance of 'Shine'.

'Johannes is my best friend,' he says. 'Although we were dancing in front of millions of people, to be honest, Johannes and I don't realise we're in front of the camera because our relationship is so strong. It was one of the first times that I really didn't think about steps but just went with the flow. It aired on the Sunday results show and the reaction from the UK audience was massive and unbelievably positive. It showed all the love that the *Strictly* family out there have for us.'

As the new celebrities gear up for their first rehearsals, Graziano has some advice for the weeks ahead: 'The celebrities are going to be ready and they're going to enjoy the vibe of *Strictly* when they start rehearsals, but then they also realise that it can be tough to keep up with a new routine every week, to be focused. The Sicilian dancer says the top priority for him is making sure the celebrities have a good time. But it's a journey and it's about doing your best. 'To me, it is not about who wins, it is about enjoying every day. Because for us, if we're lucky, we're going to be here again next year, but for the celebrities it is once and once only.'

This year, Graziano is looking forward to some innovative group numbers, which he says are the best ever. 'There is a number where we are on a rotating platform, and it was pretty hard, initially, to look comfortable and try to dance. But it is going to be spectacular!'

Caroline Quentin

Over her distinguished acting career, Caroline Quentin has starred in hit comedies, including *Men Behaving Badly* and *Kiss Me Kate*, and drama serials such as *Blue Murder* and *Jonathan Creek*. But she says the reaction to her signing for *Strictly* has outstripped all her previous work.

'I have never, in 50 years of working in showbiz, had a reaction like it to anything I've ever done,' she says. 'People are absolutely thrilled. Everywhere I go, people tell me, "We can't wait," and "We're so glad you're doing it." I've been so surprised, but until you're in the eye of the storm you don't really know how much people love something.

'I've been working with Liz Hurley and she's more excited about it than anyone I've ever met. In my local grocer, I got a round of applause when I went to buy some fruit. It's really fantastic. Honestly, if I last three and a half minutes, it's been worth it for the amazing reaction I've had.'

Cheering Caroline on through the series will be her husband, Sam, and her family, who are all thrilled that she is joining the competition.

'My husband and daughter are looking forward to it, but the one I'm most surprised by is my 17-year-old son and his friends. He's a rugby player and very sporty, and all his mates follow *Strictly Come Dancing*. They are being so sweet and so supportive and they are so excited for me.'

As a child, the Surrey-born actress went to ballet school until she was ten and has previously starred in stage musicals, but she says she has no experience of ballroom or Latin.

'I'm very excited about working one on one with a professional dancer every day, because when you do a musical, if you're a slightly older person, you tend to be taught a few steps and then dancers make you look good,' she reveals. 'But I'm actually going to learn some proper dancing skills from one of the very best people in the job.'

Having recently turned 60, Caroline says she is hoping her appearance on the show will inspire others in her age bracket.

'One of the reasons I've thought about doing it now is because we now know that as we get older we should be taxing ourselves and learning something new,' she says. 'Anything that challenges the cortex and synapses is so good for our mental well-being. I hope it encourages people of 60 and over to do a bit of dance, even if it's just on their own to a bit of music in the living room.'

The award-winning actress is also hoping her thespian skills will help her get into character for each dance, and says she's looking forward to the Tango, because 'you can use a lot of drama'.

'I'm really hoping that, having showed off for a living in all sorts of different formats, when I get to do some of the more dramatic dances, I won't be too embarrassed to really go for it. I'm going to try and use all that stuff to cover up for any nasty footwork that goes on.'

Looking to put her best foot forward, Caroline is determined she is in it to win it.

'There's little point in going into anything, whether it be a game of snap or *Strictly,* without some intention to do well, so I want to win – 100 per cent. I am going to give it my absolute best shot. If I go after week 3, at least I've tried my best and not pretended that I didn't care – because I *really* care!'

THE FINAL

After 13 weeks of mounting excitement, the Grand Final is the icing on the cake for the remaining couples.

The dance extravaganza features three routines from each finalist, including the iconic showdance. There is also the fabulous opening number which is a reunion of all of the rest of the series cast on the dance floor.

It's also the result of weeks of planning, as our behind-the-scenes look at the ultimate *Strictly* show explains.

Five weeks before the Grand Final, the teams are already coming up with ideas for the group dances, including the big reveal in the opening number, when the finalists are unveiled.

'We like to make it as spectacular a reveal for them as possible,' says Series Director Nikki Parsons. 'Last year we did a laser show, with the three finalists lit up on podiums at the end.

has something spectacular. For example, in series 17, Kelvin Fletcher had a huge jukebox, Karim Zeroual had a beautiful light show and a shower of glitter and Emma Barton had a golden stage with staircases down the side.

'The routine comes together in an organic process between the dancers and all of us, so we start working on it at the Quarter-final stage. Then, once we know which couples have made the Final, we can just sign off on the big builds so they can start to be made.'

Final Week

By the time the Semi-final is over the teams have done much of the prep for the Grand Final.

'Throughout the series, we're working a week in advance,' explains Executive Producer Sarah James. 'So on the week of the Final, it's great that we can put all our energy into that one last show and not have to plan ahead for the following week.'

For Jason Gilkison, it's a busy week as he oversees the opening number as well as putting together a fabulous routine for the

Planning starts early for that.'

As soon as the Quarter-finals are over, a week before the finalists are revealed, Executive Producer Sarah James, Creative Director Jason Gilkison, the Music Producer and the dance team begin holding meetings with the professional dancers about the all-important showdances.

'We want them to be real wow moments and often they involve a big prop build or a spectacular set,' says Sarah. 'So we talk about what styles of dance they might want their showdance to include, ideas for props or a big entrance that they might want for their celebrity and any big special effects.

'We try to make sure it's fair so that everybody

returning celebrities, often working with other choreographers.

'The pros that have been eliminated go straight into creating the opening number, which is a summing up of the entire season, ending in the incredible reveal of the finalists,' he says.

'We work on that on Monday and Tuesday, without our finalists because they're in rehearsal.'

On Wednesday, the eliminated celebrities come together to learn their final group number.

'We normally do a routine that includes hints and highlights of each person's journey, such as bringing back the horse that Jeremy Vine started his Salsa on,' says Jason.

'They are so hyper and excited to see each other that it takes them an hour to settle down. It's like herding cats, but it's such a fun day.'

Final Friday

On Friday, the finalists rehearse their three routines in the studio for the first time.

'It's a big day for the finalists, because they have to camera-block three numbers, repeating each one three times, which is pretty intense,' says Jason.

'It requires a lot of stamina, so we try to mix it up and give them a break in between.'

Sarah and Nikki watch the rehearsals from the production gallery, noting down any last-minute production tweaks they might like to make.

'Everybody who reaches the Final feels like they've already won in a way, because they've completed the journey,' says Sarah. 'So the atmosphere is always electric on that Friday and Saturday.'

The Big Day

8AM

Sarah, Nikki and the production team tend to arrive early at the studio and immediately begin rehearsals for the big group number.

'At this point, we start seeing the costumes for the dances, so we're getting a really good idea of how everything's going to look with props, costume and lighting,' says Sarah.

'I make any necessary tweaks, not to the choreography but to the lighting and graphics and how the number feels. Nikki and I work closely together on what shots are taken.'

The dancers and celebrities also arrive early, flitting between hair and make-up and the costume department and putting the finishing touches on their final looks in between rehearsal time.

The whole day is planned out like a military operation, with spreadsheets dictating where each dancer and celebrity needs to be at any given moment, as well as Tess and Claudia.

'There's a huge grid showing when people need to be in make-up and wardrobe, in the studio rehearsing, having physio, etcetera,' says Sarah.

'Then each couple has a runner allocated to them, who is constantly on a headset, running around backstage and making sure everyone is where they need to be at the right time.'

10AM

After the two group numbers, the couples get time to rehearse with the band for the first time.

'They each get two run-throughs, but we leave a bit longer for the showdances because they are new numbers, unlike the favourite and the judges' choice, which they have danced before,' says Sarah.

Tess and Claudia arrive mid-morning and, after saying hello and good luck to all the finalists, head to their dressing rooms for hair and make-up.

1PM

Lunch break.

2PM

The dress rehearsal begins, bringing all the elements of the live show together for the first time, with full costume, hair and make-up, props and the live band.

The only people missing are the audience and the judges, who are replaced by stand-ins from the production team so there's no sneak peak of the routines before the real thing.

Again, Sarah and Nikki watch the rehearsal from the gallery and, when the run-through is over, the production team get together for one final meeting.

'I go through the changes we want to hair or make-up, costume, lighting or graphics with the various teams, then they go and deliver those notes to the departments,' says Sarah.

'But at this point it's nothing major, because we have to make sure there's enough time to turn it around for the live show.'

5PM

The live audience, who have been waiting patiently, begin to file in to the studio and the level of excitement rises even more.

Warm-up man Stuart Holdham comes on the studio floor to whip up the crowd and brief them on what will happen in the show, then Tess and Claudia join him, to say hello to the studio audience ahead of the show.

7PM

The production crew, audience and presenters are all in their places as the iconic theme tune begins to play.

'Everyone's so excited on a Saturday night anyway, hyped up for a live show,' says Nikki. 'We always clap along to the titles in the gallery to get our energy going, but on the Grand Final night, that steps up a gear.

'We know it's the last one, there's a huge amount of content and we're all invested in the celebrities, so we're all keen to see who will win.'

Having all the cast from the whole series back on set, adds to the buzz in the air.

'By the Semi-final there's only four or five couples left' says Jason. 'Then all of a sudden everybody's back and it feels so full again – and loads of fun.'

As soon as the first dances are over, the public vote opens and a polling company, working in a separate room at the studio, begin the count, watched over by independent verifiers.

'The moment when the lines shut and we count up to find out the winner is so exciting,' says Sarah.

'Then we have to turn around the result quickly and get the cue cards out to the presenters during the VTs and group dances so they can reveal the result.'

With the tears of joy, hugs and congratulations, it's time to bring the show to a close and to celebrate.

But for Jason, the whole day has the atmosphere of a party.

'Everybody is glad to get to the Final and the whole day feels like a wonderful celebration.'

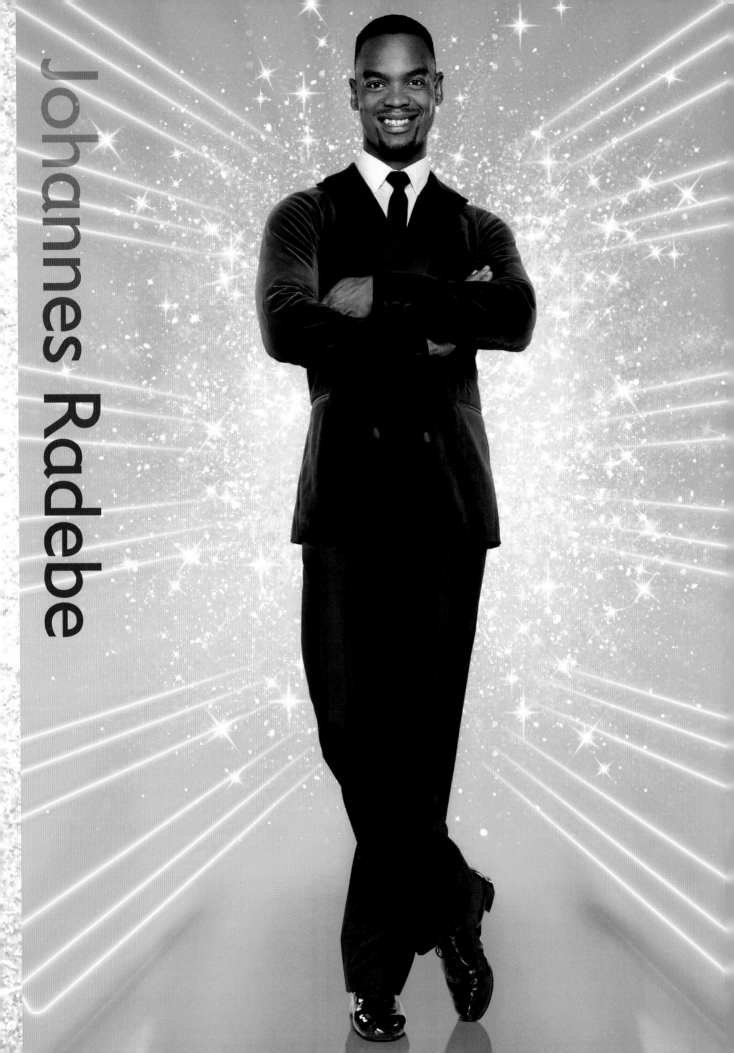

Johannes Radebe

South African pro Johannes Radebe danced with his first celebrity partner, Catherine Tyldesley, in series 17 and can't wait to get back in the ballroom.

'I feel so fortunate to be dancing again and, for me, coming back to *Strictly* is everything,' he says. 'I'm looking forward to meeting my partner. It's going be an interesting ride and I'm excited to make a new friend.'

Born in Zamdela, Sasolburg, in South Africa, Johannes took up dancing at seven and competed in provincial Latin competitions as a child. At 20, he joined the Afro Arimba Dance Company and has since become two-time Professional South African Latin Champion and three-time South African Amateur Latin Champion. Before joining the professional team on the UK's *Strictly* in 2018, he performed in two seasons of the South African show, reaching the Grand Final on both occasions.

As well as competing on *Strictly* last year, Johannes danced a memorable same-sex dance with Graziano Di Prima, to Emeli Sandé's 'Shine'.

'Graziano and I dance together all the time, and having the opportunity to do it on that dance floor was, for me, another day at work with my best friend,' he says. 'It was just a beautiful experience for me.'

As he prepares to meet his 2020 celebrity, Johannes says he is looking to make it a fun experience.

'More than anything, I want her to really enjoy the experience, because this is a once-in-a-lifetime opportunity for the celebrities,' he says. 'I want them to come in really wanting to learn this skill and I want them to fall in love with dancing through this competition. I think they will all be competitive, but I also want them to believe they can do this.'

With the right teacher and the right attitude, Johannes believes anyone can learn to dance.

'The student has got to learn what the teacher gives them but take it further by practising and making it better, so they can take what they've learned to the next level,' he says. 'It's about pushing the boundaries and it's up to the students as well as the teacher.'

While he will push his pupil to help her improve, Johannes says he is a kind teacher.

'Over the years I've learnt patience above anything,' he says. 'I've been dancing and teaching for years, but to someone who has never heard of a Cha-cha-cha, it's a very daunting experience. So I am a very patient teacher, but, at the same time, I know how to get results. I push when I have to push, but I do it nicely. We all have to have fun.'

Catherine was a model pupil and, despite being eliminated at Halloween, his first year partnering a celebrity was a dream for Johannes.

'I got such a lot of support and advice from other pros,' he says. 'They help each other out and I could bounce ideas off them, so I really felt supported. To have been partnered with the kindest, sweetest person in Catherine set me up nicely, too. She did her homework, practising what I taught her in class and sending me videos, and she was very dedicated. She was bitten by the dancing bug early on and I loved that. My journey was honestly incredible.

'Of course, I wanted to make it to the Final so that she could dance every week, but hey, it's a competition.

'I'm determined to go further this year. I am going for solid gold! I am on it! I've seen how it's done. Now, reset. Let's do it again!'

Ranvir Singh

As *Good Morning Britain*'s political editor, Ranvir Singh is used to the pressures of live TV and thinking on her feet. But being in the *Strictly* spotlight will be a whole new experience.

'I'm always the one asking the questions and the spotlight is definitely not on me,' she says. 'It's on the issue or on the person I'm talking to. But personal confidence has come later on in life with me and, at 43, I'm more relaxed about being me. I'm looking forward to people seeing me in a different light. I like to laugh a lot, and you don't really get to laugh a lot when you're reporting on politics every day, so I'm looking forward to having a fun time.'

When it comes to dancing, Ranvir had a brief taste as a child, but it wasn't her finest hour. 'I did proudly do Grade 1 ballet when I was seven,' she says. 'But my dance career ended after my teacher put in my report card, "Ranvir is enthusiastic but sadly lands like an elephant." She said that I'd never be able to go en pointe, so there was no point carrying on. Maybe with *Strictly*, I can heal that scar – 36 years later, I'm picking up my dance career!'

Despite her early experience, the *GMB* star is not shy of the dance floor at family parties.

'My family, who have seen me do Bhangra, are confident that I have a sense of rhythm,' she says. 'But the ballroom is a far cry from bopping around at a wedding. I'm not stiff, which is a good thing. I can jingle-jangle around a little bit and hopefully the teacher can show me how to control that.'

Preston-born Ranvir started her journalistic career on BBC Radio Lancashire and BBC Greater Manchester before moving on to local TV stations. In 2012, she joined ITV's *Daybreak* and, two years later, became one of the founding team on *GMB*. She has also been an ITN news reader and recently fronted *Loose Women*.

For advice, Ranvir has been turning to her *GMB* co-stars, who have already had the *Strictly* experience.

'Susanna Reid's immediate advice was at all costs to try and avoid the Cha-cha-cha and the Samba, but I don't know if I can avoid them,' she says. 'She said, "You have no idea what is about to happen. You're about to be in the centre of a complete whirlwind." Kate Garraway said, "Don't miss the opportunity to hit the ground running and take training seriously from the beginning." Charlotte Hawkins and Richard Arnold have also done it and everybody says, "This is going to be the best thing you've ever done. Enjoy every second."'

The busy presenter will be fitting her training and performances around a packed schedule of TV work but says Olympic gold medallist Nicola Adams has given her a top tip for keeping the energy levels up.

'Nicola said she can sleep anywhere,' says Ranvir. 'So I'm going to take every chance I get to have a nap, to give me a burst of energy.'

Having never played competitive sport, Ranvir says she is lacking the competitive streak – and will be cheering on her fellow contestants to win. 'I am the least sporty person, so it just makes me cry with laughter that I am now competing against an Olympic gold-medal-winning boxer,' she says. 'I'm literally the least competitive person you've ever met. It's embarrassing! If I play Scrabble, I'm like, "Show me your letter and I'll help you get a really good word." I want everyone to do really well for themselves.

'On the other hand, the day after I was announced my niece spent 25 minutes telling me how excited she was about Jamie Laing being in the show, because she loves him. So I'm not sure she will vote for me!'

Ranvir says she is grateful to be offered the new challenge and is looking forward to learning a new skill. 'My family have been super excited and my friends are beside themselves,' she says. 'I'm just aware of how lucky I am to be asked to be part of it, because everybody is so happy about it. Before the show is even on air it's spreading joy. The 12 of us are probably the luckiest people in Britain right now.'

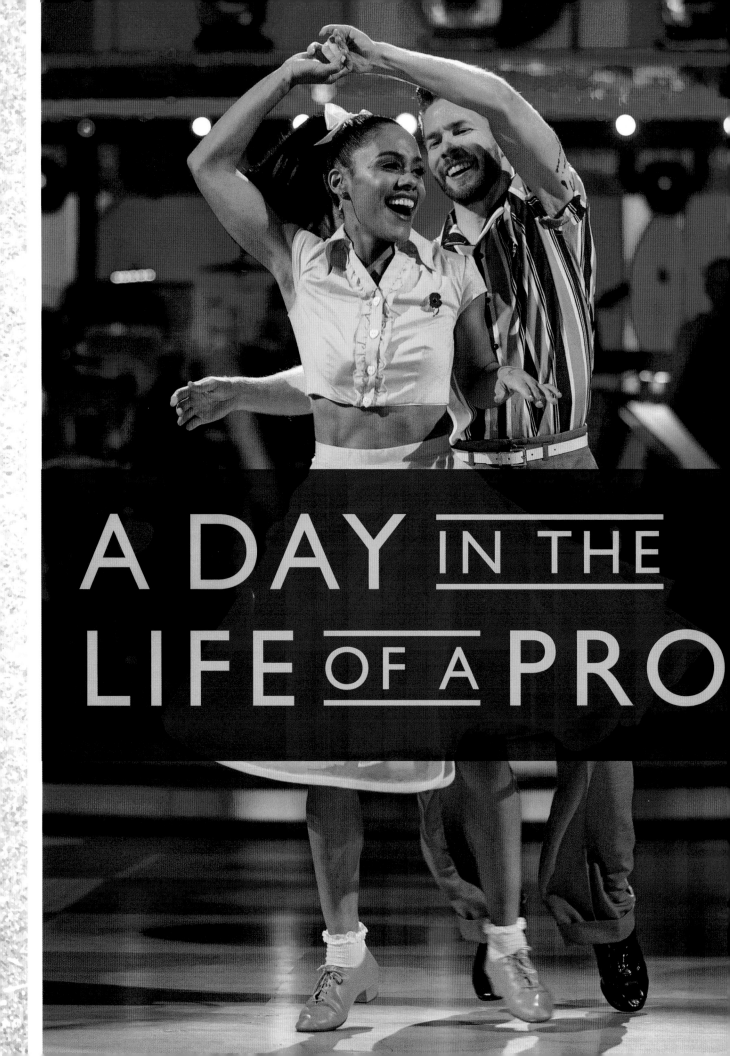

A DAY IN THE LIFE OF A PRO

During the run of the series, the pros are working flat out to get their celebrity partners ready for the live show. Here, two of the show's dancers, Neil Jones and Oti Mabuse, talk us through a typical day in the life of a *Strictly* professional.

Neil Jones

A *STRICTLY* WORKING WEEK WITH ALEX SCOTT ON SERIES 17

I typically got up at around 7am on a rehearsal day, walked the dog and then headed straight to the studio. I usually bought a bagel and a shake or a juice for my dance partner and I on the way to the studio and then we'd eat that when we arrived at 9am while we chatted things through.

On a Monday, we'd discuss the weekend's show, how the dance went, the results show and the judges' comments. Once we'd put the previous week to rest I'd then ask Alex how she was feeling about the dance we were about to do.

During the run, I'd spend Sundays creating the routine as I can't walk into the rehearsal room on Monday morning thinking, 'What will I do?' I need to feel confident I have a finished routine ready to teach.

On Monday we'd start learning the dance by standing side by side and I'd show Alex every step she'd be dancing that week. The ambition would be that by the end of Monday we'd have worked through the entire routine at least once as well as tried it to music.

When we're in training we try not to break until lunchtime and then I think it's a good idea to get an hour out of the studio to go for a walk, get some fresh air and a bite to eat.

Typically, we'd eat a high-protein lunch such as avocado on toast with chicken or a chicken salad – nothing too heavy as otherwise we'd struggle to dance again in the afternoon.

If the VT team want to ask questions or interview the celebrity, they would usually do that in a scheduled break, often after lunch, which is great as often we didn't want to dance straight away and were happy to talk until were ready to start dancing and training again.

We don't know when the camera crews are coming. They could be there all day or just for a couple of hours but they're brilliant and could film our training with us hardly noticing that they were – it's all part of the *Strictly* experience.

Last year with Alex I found that in the afternoon we'd often forget the time and just keep going. The only thing we stop for is a cup of tea and a snack to keep the energy levels up. Also while I'd normally finish at around 8pm, with Alex last year, we tried to do more and could often go on until 10 p.m. On Mondays, we wouldn't leave until she knew the dance or at least had a really good understanding of it, as we found that worked well for us.

When I got home, I'd look through a video of the last dance of the day and write notes on where we'd got work to do the following day.

With the celebrity knowing the steps by Monday, I spent Tuesday on the fundamentals of the technique and we'd dance the whole routine to music – however good or bad.

By Wednesday we'd aim to be in a position to start working on the detail. For example if anything was flagged in the judges' comments the week before, you particularly try to nail those areas.

On Thursday, we'd work on the performance and go through the whole routine all day. Thursdays are full on, but hopefully, if we were confident on where we were at, we'd finish around 7pm so we were rested and ready for the studio rehearsals on Friday and the main event on Saturday.

Oti Mabuse

A *STRICTLY* SATURDAY

On a *Strictly* Saturday I wake at 3am – not because of nerves, but because I always wake at that time. I plan my day, go over the dance and the little things we still have to fix. I also think about the message I am going to send my celebrity when I get up, usually something like, 'We can do this. We've got each other's backs.' I want that message of encouragement to be the first thing they see in the morning, so they know it's going to be a good day.

After another short sleep, I get up, shower and go for breakfast at the hotel in Elstree where we stay after Friday rehearsals. Breakfast is the biggest meal of the day for me, because we burn a lot of energy on a show day. A typical breakfast is scrambled eggs, avocado on toast and porridge with blueberries and a spoonful of peanut butter.

We are given a call time when we have to be on set, which is usually between 9am and 10am I go straight into make-up for 45 minutes, which gives them time to do the full face that will last the whole day, with touch-ups. It also has to be a look that can work for the opening group number, the couple's dance, the opening number of the results show and then our dance again – four different looks in a day! The make-up team do a really good job, and sometimes they will do just the eyes and the foundation so they can change the lipstick and eyebrows, or they'll change the eyes. It's incredible how they create a completely different look for every occasion.

After make-up comes the band call, when we hear the band play the music for the first time that week. We have two run-throughs of the routine, which are crucial because often the song sounds different to the rehearsal track, so it can throw the celebrities.

Lunch is usually chicken with rice and vegetables or salad, eaten in the make-up chair as I get ready for the full dress rehearsal.

The dress run begins with the opening pro number, which we first learned in group rehearsals in August, and we go through that twice. Then it's back to hair, make-up and costume to be transformed for the couple's dance.

Throughout the day the quick changes mean that hair, make-up and costume are all working on you at once, sometimes as many as six people, with someone also doing your nails, which have to change colour for every number.

I usually have my hair in braids to protect it, and then the stylist uses wigs or extensions to change the colour and style.

Now dressed and ready for the couple's dance, we do the dress run of the whole show, which brings us up to dinnertime. Because I'll be dancing, dinner needs to be light – usually a chicken salad. The food on set is really good, and I save some for after I've danced, to keep my energy up.

Before the show, I pray. I also have a ritual that involves hairbands on my wrist, which I snap when I'm nervous. Every time I snap them, I say, 'You've got this. It's going to be a good performance.' Every performance is unique, fresh and so exciting. But there are also nerves, and on top of that I have to make sure my partner, who has never danced before, is not nervous and remembers the routine.

After another stint in hair and make-up, we change into the opening-number costumes and go onto the floor to dance it in front of the audience and cameras. Then it's a quick change backstage for the couple's dance, last-minute style changes, and I meet up with my celebrity for a quick warm-up and a little pep talk. We're told our performance order before the live show.

Personally, I prefer to dance towards the end of the show, which gives me prep time, warm-up time and more time to talk with my partner. I like to know how they're feeling, if they're nervous, and to get my thoughts and my energy together for the dance.

After the show, there are more quick changes to film the opening number for the results show, before getting back into our couple's look for the elimination.

We finish at about midnight and I head home. After an exciting show, I'm still running on adrenaline and emotion, so I have to calm down and relax. I take a shower or soak in the bath, then I'm rested and ready to do it all again next week – as long as we made it through!

Ian Waite

As a former *Strictly* pro dancer, Ian Waite is the voice of authority when it comes to handing out tips to the competing celebrities on *It Takes Two*.

Every week, in Waite's Warm-Up, he casts an expert eye over the couples' rehearsal tapes and uses his unique telestrator and his magic wand to point out the technique the celebrities are mastering and the areas to work on.

'I just love doing the Warm-Up because I get to see all the couples' choreography on film before anybody else in the country and pick the bits that I want to talk about,' he says. 'The telestrator is a great aid because I can circle round elbows and legs to illustrate my points. I also get to demonstrate with Zoe Ball, which I love because she's such a great dancer.'

Ian and *ITT* presenter Zoe have been the best of friends since they danced together on *Strictly* in 2005, making it all the way to the Final. But, Ian reveals, they met the year before. 'Zoe interviewed me,' he says. 'I told her she should do *Strictly Come Dancing* and she said, "I couldn't do that. I'm too lazy and I eat crisps and chocolate." We did a little dance and she got it all wrong. But after that she signed up for *Strictly* and, then the producers put us together, which was a lovely surprise.' Now, 15 years on, the pair are reunited every year to talk dance on *It Takes Two*.

'It's a great excuse to see each other,' he says. 'We get the chance to chat about everyday stuff and catch up. It doesn't feel like work, to be honest, because we both enjoy it so much. It's just two friends gossiping.'

The addition of Rylan Clark-Neal to *ITT* last year has added to the party feel of the show, says Ian. 'I think he's brilliant. He's so quick-witted, fast and funny, which is perfect for our show, because it's a fun show. We all have a laugh and it's a real family, so he fits in perfectly.'

Originally from Reading, Berkshire, Ian started dancing at the age of 10 when his dad insisted he took his five-year-old brother along to classes. After two months of watching from the sidelines, Ian was persuaded to get on the floor and fell in love with dance. At 14, he was crowned European Youth Latin American Champion. After turning professional in 1997, he moved to the Netherlands, where he became Dutch Champion and reached the finals of both the World Showdance Championship and the European Professional Latin American Championship. After five years, he returned to the UK and began dancing with Camilla Dallerup, joining *Strictly* in 2004 and making the Final with athlete Denise Lewis. Other celebrity partners have included Penny Lancaster, Mica Paris and Jade Johnson.

'*Strictly* looks completely different now to when I first joined,' he comments. 'We had just tables and chairs, a curtain at the back and a few lights. It's so much more visual, with LED screens around the studio, amazing lighting and props. We didn't have themes, although I often made them up anyway. Then props and storytelling came in and themed weeks like Movie Week and Musicals Week – which is my personal favourite.

'The show has evolved so much and I think that's why it's still so popular.'

But working on *ITT* means he remains close to the show, and he says he has fond memories of his time on the *Strictly* floor. 'My favourite moments were making the Final twice with Denise and Zoe, and also the two dances I did with Darcey Bussell, in 2010 and 2012. She asked if I would partner her, which was a dream come true because I was a massive fan. I also danced a Viennese Waltz in front of Shirley Bassey and performed in front of the Spice Girls. You can't beat those moments and they'll always be special.'

GO PRO!

Dancing on the show and on tour keeps *Strictly*'s professional dancers superfit, but when they're not dancing daily, they have other ways to keep fit.

Here, Karen Hauer and Gorka Márquez talk us through their fitness routines and share their tips for keeping in tip-top condition.

Karen Hauer

When I'm not on the show, I usually work out six days a week, depending on how my body's feeling, which I think is one of the most important things. When I wake up, I have to decide if I'm feeling good enough to do the workout that I want to do or whether I need to modify it.

My workouts are intensive bursts of energy, lasting about 15 to 20 minutes a day, with exercises based around balance, core, strength training and agility. All the exercises that I do use bodyweight, rather than dumbbells and other equipment, although I sometimes use a skipping rope.

For us, it's not about the way we look but about working on imbalances that we have in our bodies, making sure that we're strengthening and lengthening muscles to prevent injuries and enhancing weaker muscles to make sure we minimise any aches and pains that dancing may cause.

I don't go to the gym, because I prefer working out at home in my own environment and, being a professional dancer, I don't get a lot of time to spend at home. I have shifted my entire living room to create a little workout space, which is perfect, but it does mean that my three dogs often get involved!

My diet is another way that I look after my health. I eat everything, but it is always home cooked. I do love a plate full of vegetables, I love salmon and chicken and I only eat meat once a week. I love soups, Greek yoghurt with fruit and bagels with peanut butter – all food that will give me energy throughout the day so my sugar levels don't drop dramatically. I can't afford to be hungry, because then I can't be productive and I get 'hangry'!

When I want to indulge myself, I dig in to milk chocolate – the big bars, not the little ones. I also love truffle crisps and always have some in my drawer – and even under my bed.

During the *Strictly* run, I don't work out because I'm on my feet nine hours a day, so I need to make sure that I rest enough after rehearsals. Similarly, when I'm on tour I'm fully immersed in the show for at least two hours, so I make sure I give my body enough time to recover.

My tip to anyone who wants to start working out is to make sure that they listen to their bodies at all times and not overdo things. I recommend short, sharp bursts that get the heart rate up, increase stamina and strengthen the core.

Karen's 15-minute workout

Do three rounds of the following exercises, working for 40 seconds and resting for 20 seconds on each exercise. Don't forget to breathe and have fun!

Side shuffle and tap – Shuffle to the left three times, then reach down with your right hand to tap the floor, then shuffle back to the right and tap. Repeat for 40 seconds.

Reverse lunges – To work the bottom and leg muscles. Stand with feet hip-width apart, then step backwards with your right leg until your knees are at a 90-degree angle, with your right knee pointing towards the ground and in line with your toes. Push yourself forward to the start position and repeat with your left leg.

Lying hip raises – This is great for your hamstrings, butt, lower back and core. Lie on your back with your knees bent and raise your hips until your body forms a straight line from shoulders to knees. Slowly lower and repeat.

High plank marching – Adopt a push-up position with your legs stretched back and your hands on the floor. Then raise alternate legs and bring them down to tap on the floor, as if marching on the balls of your feet.

The 100 – Lie on your back and bring your legs up to a 45-degree angle. Then bring your upper body up into a crunch and place your arms by your side. Move your arms up and down very quickly.

Gorka Márquez

When I'm not on *Strictly* I train six times a week, taking the whole day off on Sunday. On Wednesday I concentrate on conditioning or aerobic work, without the usual weight training. My garage at home is converted into a gym, with all the fitness equipment I need, so I work out there for 30 minutes to 1 hour 15 minutes per session.

There are two parts to my daily training – strength and aerobic resistance. Many people think dancers don't need to train, but strength is important because there are lots of tricks and lifts. For example, we might be doing overhead powerlifts and jumps, possibly from a platform to the floor, so strength helps to avoid injury.

My first routine includes bodyweight exercises such as squats, heavy exercises with barbells, bench presses and shoulder presses. I also do plyometric exercises like jumping onto a box and forward jumps using my body weight.

The second session is focused on my aerobic/anaerobic capacity. It is very important for a dancer to have good aerobic resistance for long periods of dance, but also to maintain performance during different rhythms and styles, switching from fast to slow dances.

When you have to perform a high-energy dance for three minutes you want to look fresh and happy, not like you're struggling. So I use aerobic equipment like the bike or rowing machine to train for aerobic capacity, or how long you can work at the higher range of your heart rate, between 120 and 140 beats per second.

Some sessions are steady work between 120/140rpm and others use interval training, working at peaks of 160/170rpm. That helps my lungs get used to a high volume of work and cope with the peaks and troughs of energy output during shows.

I think of myself as an athlete, so I train like one. I might work out in the morning and go for a 5km run in the afternoon.

During the *Strictly* run, or when I am on tour, I'm dancing for long hours, so my workout is more for maintenance and recovery. I do stretches and short sessions after the show, so my body feels ready for the next week. It's similar to a footballer who trains

hardest off season and then, during the season, they train more lightly for recovery and strength, to keep the body healthy.

Food wise, I like to eat a good balance of vitamins and minerals. I don't eat pork or red meat, so it's mostly chicken or fish with legumes, like kidney beans, and a lot of greens. The only sugar I have is natural sugar, from greens and fruit. I love to cook and everything I eat is cooked from scratch because I like to know what food I am putting on the table. But I do love my pizza, so that's my big treat!

Gorka's 15-minute workout

Repeat each exercise for 20 seconds with a 10-second break for a full-body workout. Start with three or four rounds of each and add more when you can.

Burpees – Begin in a standing position, then squat with your hands on the ground. Shift your weight to your arms and jump your feet back into a plank position. Return to squat position and jump into the air, raising your arms.

Bodyweight squats – Start with your feet shoulder-width apart, toes slightly turned out and arms stretched out in front of you. Bend your knees and drop your hips to lower your body, keeping your heels on the floor. Push back up to the starting position.

Forward lunges – Stand with your feet shoulder-width apart and take a big stride with your right leg, keeping the torso upright. Bend the right leg until the thigh is parallel to the floor and the calf is vertical. Push back to standing and repeat with the left leg.

Walkout push-ups – Start on your feet, bend at the waist and place your hands on the floor. Walk your hands out until you are in a plank position, then do a push up and walk your hands back to your feet and return to standing.

Isometric plank – Rest on your elbows with your legs stretched out behind you so that your body forms a straight line from your head to your feet. Hold for 20 seconds.

STRICTLY CROSSWORD

Across

1. Traditional ballroom dance in 4/4 time (7)
3. Where 11 down is called to – or a place to meet for after-show drinks (3, 3)
6. Series 12 contestant, Thom (5)
8. – – – – 'n' Roll, American-style dance (4)
9. What *Strictly Come Dancing* is (7)
10. Mr Judd, winner of series nine (5)
12. Former tennis player and breakfast presenter who took part in series 9 (3, 4)
14. Series 16 finalist, Ashley (7)
16. – – – – – ball, another name for a glitterball (5)
18. See 23 across (7)
21. Russian pro, Ms Mushtuk (4)
22. Ballroom dance with two variations danced on *Strictly* (5)
23. And 18 across. Female professional dancer who hails from Australia (6)
24. Davood Ghadami danced his Argentine Tango as this character from an Andrew Lloyd Webber musical in series 15.

Down

1. The surname of the series 17 winner (8)
2. Alex Scott danced a Jive to 'Let's – – – – – Again' in series 17 (5)
3. To rotate in a dance (4)
4. Series 8 finalist, Matt (5)
5. Shared surname of two female contestants in series 10 and 11 (5)
7. Charles Aznavour classic that Anton du Beke and Patsy Palmer chose for their Rumba (3)
11. Judge Rinder's first name (3)
13. Where the dancing takes place (8)
15. First name of the pro who lifted the trophy with 1 down in 2019 (3)
16. First name of *Strictly*'s band leader, Mr Arch (5)
17. Dance of Cuban origin, which became popular in the US in the 1950s (5)
18. Style of jazz that had its heyday in the 1940s (5)
19. The inside of the *Strictly* studio (3)
20. Stick often used as a prop in routines (4)

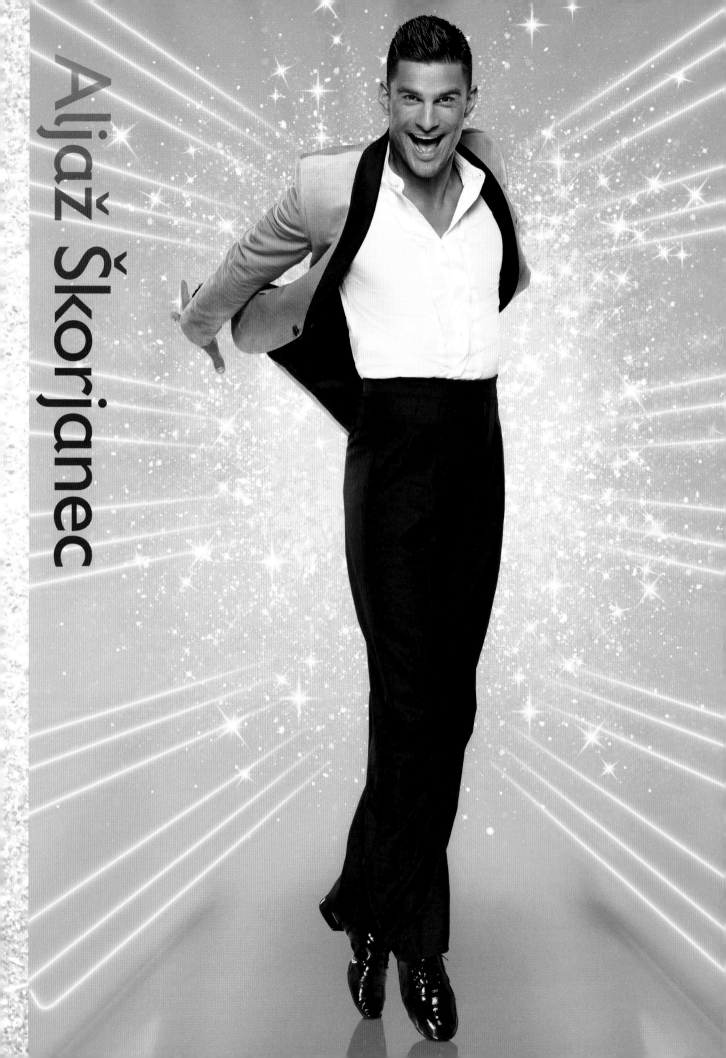

Aljaž Škorjanec

Former *Strictly* champ Aljaž Škorjanec will be looking to add another glitterball to his mantelpiece this year, but initially he's just excited about getting his teacher's hat on and welcoming his latest pupil.

'What I'm most looking forward to this year is taking someone who has or hasn't danced before, and teaching them my way of doing ballroom and Latin,' he says. 'I can't wait to teach someone again. I'm so excited to get going, to see a happy face when they get something right, to see a frustrated face when they're *trying* to get it right. That's what I love the most about *Strictly* every year.'

The Slovenian dancer is keen for his celebrity partner to have fun during their *Strictly* run but is also expecting some high standards.

'I always want my celebrity to come into *Strictly* having really high expectations of themselves,' he says. 'I want them to be willing to work hard. Then, in return, I'm going to make sure that they leave with the best feeling that they've ever had about anything that they've ever done. I want them to enjoy themselves and have fun, while they're pushing themselves the hardest they ever have.'

Aljaž was brought up in a small town in Slovenia where he started dancing at the age of five. He went on to become 19-time Slovenian champion in ballroom, Latin and Ten Dance. He joined *Strictly* in 2013 and made his mark in the first year, sweeping to victory with model and TV presenter Abbey Clancy in the first all-female Final in the show's history. Since then, his partners have included Alison Hammond, Helen George and Daisy Lowe, and in 2017, he made the Final again with actress Gemma Atkinson. Last year he reached week 7 with Emma Weymouth, who runs the Longleat country estate with her husband, the Marquess of Bath.

'Emma was absolutely lovely, so kind and caring,' he says. 'I haven't rehearsed outside of London since Alison Hammond, in 2014, and I got to spend time in Warminster and at Longleat, so it was so lovely to be there and enjoy that magical place.'

This year, Aljaž is lining up some spectacular choreography for his latest celebrity, and says he's been taking inspiration from many sources. 'The preparation for the next series of *Strictly* never stops, so I've been picking out songs, looking back at videos of all those amazing professional couples from the past, doing some research. It's great inspiration for the upcoming series, which I do every year to come up with new ideas, but I always tailor choreography, songs and ideas to my celebrities. So as soon as I find out who my celebrity is, I begin to think how I'm going to approach the routines, and every year I approach them completely differently.'

Whoever he's dancing with, Aljaž hopes he and the other pros and celebrities will bring a collective smile to the nation. 'That's what we are there for,' he says. 'Obviously the show is about celebrities dancing, doing something they have never done before, so it's interesting to watch. But essentially it is a show that makes people smile. That's what we're aiming for and we can't wait for that Saturday-night feeling.'

Jacqui Smith

Former minister Jacqui Smith is the fourth politician to swap the ballot box for the ballroom on the show, and she's been taking tips from one of the most memorable *Strictly* alumni.

'I've been lucky that Ed Balls has talked to me and given me some advice,' she says. 'I'm not sure that I would ever be able to match his "Gangnam Style" dance, but I should replay the video and watch very carefully. He gave me some really important advice, which is that people love *Strictly* and they love you taking it seriously and trying hard, so that's absolutely what I'm going to be doing.'

Although Jacqui has had no formal training, she is already the proud owner of a bronze medal for dancing – which she won when she was seven.

'My mother took me to Scottish Highland dance classes, and I got a bronze medal for dancing a Highland fling and a sword dance,' she reveals. 'It's not like I came third in a competition, it's just a basic qualification that you get at that age. But I was one of the first up on the dance floor at discos and family parties when I was younger. That's about it when it comes to my experience.'

As a relative novice, Jacqui says she will need to start with the basics, but she was never in any doubt that she wanted to take on the *Strictly* challenge.

'The opportunity to have a new adventure at my age, to learn something completely new from the best teachers and dancers in the country, seemed like a fantastic opportunity,' she says.

Born in Worcestershire, Jacqui trained and worked as a teacher before entering politics. She was elected Labour MP for Redditch in 1997 and served in various government roles, including Minister of State for Schools, before becoming the UK's first female Home Secretary in 2007. Since leaving politics in 2010, she has served as chair to an NHS trust in Birmingham,

the Jo Cox Foundation and the Sandwell Children's Trust, as well as hosting a weekly show on LBC. Having signed up to *Strictly*, she says the reaction from colleagues and family has been incredible.

'People have been absolutely delighted, whether it's at the trusts where I work or my family and friends,' she says. 'I always knew that *Strictly* brought joy to people, but I haven't seen it first-hand and it's been absolutely lovely.

'My youngest son is the first person I told. He said, "That's absolutely brilliant," and he's been really positive ever since. My sisters are very excited, but they are also helping me to keep my feet on the ground. My mum is a relatively new *Strictly* fan – I introduced her to it – so she's very excited as well.'

Jacqui jokes that her biggest competition is 'the dance floor', but says the other 11 contestants make an impressive line-up.

'They seem fabulous. They all look to me as if they could be fit and quite good dancers,' she says. 'I know Ranvir Singh already and we've been messaging each other. So I think it's going to be absolutely brilliant and I'm really looking forward to meeting them.'

While she's keen to try all the dances, the former MP is most looking forward to trying the Tango. 'I was fortunate enough to see a Tango in a Buenos Aires Tango bar,' she says. 'It's something that has stayed with me forever and the opportunity to do something like that would be absolutely amazing.'

She is also first in line for the tanning booth and ready to embrace the *Strictly* makeover. 'Having tried to put on fake tan each summer and have it go all streaky, I'm very much looking forward to a proper spray tan, which I've never had before,' she says. 'Everybody knows that the wardrobe and make-up teams are absolutely fantastic, so having them look after me is going to be amazing.'

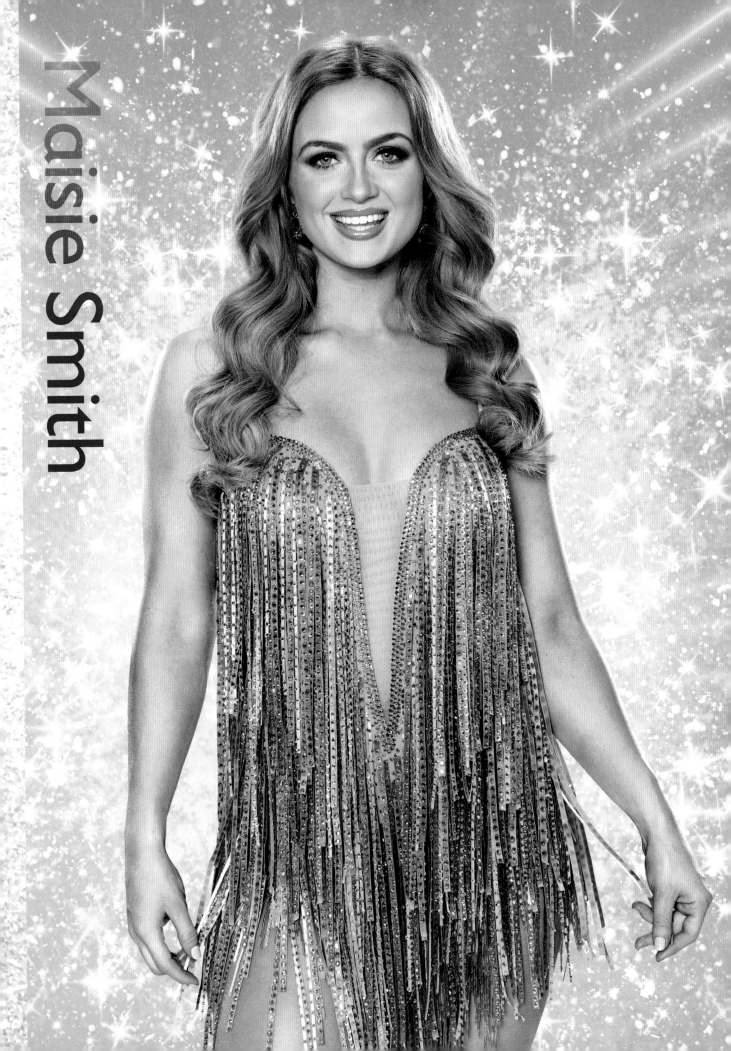

Maisie Smith

Having had a tiny taste of *Strictly* magic when she won the 2019 Children in Need special with Kevin Clifton, Maisie Smith is hungry for more.

The *EastEnders* actress has been a fan of the show since she was a little girl and says competing in the series is a dream come true.

'*Strictly* is a family favourite and I don't think there's anyone who hasn't seen the show,' she says. 'My mum and I have been watching it since forever and it's a dream of ours. I told my mum as soon as I got the phone call – she was the first person I thought of. She has wanted me to do it and she had her fingers crossed since I did the Children in Need special, so she was over the moon!

'It's one of those things that you always wanted to do, but you don't expect it to actually happen. So in my house there was a lot of shock, but everyone is so excited. It's been a really happy vibe at work and at home and with everyone.'

Born in Essex, Maisie was a child actress who played the young Elizabeth I in *The Other Boleyn Girl* before joining *EastEnders* as Tiffany Dean, at the age of six. The actress follows in the *Strictly* footsteps of many of her cast mates, including screen mum Patsy Palmer, and says she has had plenty of advice from all of them.

'There's often been someone from *EastEnders* on the show, who I can support, and now that I'm that person it's just surreal,' she says. 'A lot of them have said, "Enjoy it. It's going to be hard and it will take a lot out of you, but remember to have the best time and be yourself," which is the perfect advice.'

After watching co-star Emma Barton sweep to the Final last year, Maisie says she is looking forward to a *Strictly* makeover.

'That is genuinely what I think I'm most excited about – being glammed up every single week!' she says. 'I remember when Emma did it last year. I barely do scenes with her so when I do see her it's usually as her character, Honey. But watching her every week on *Strictly*, she just looked incredible and I can't wait for them to work that magic on me.'

Maisie says she loves hitting the dance floor at a party – and busting some moves runs in the family.

'Me, my mum and my sister are like a trio to watch out for on the dance floor,' she says. 'At least, that's how we see each other. We're a pretty dancey family and all love a bit of musical theatre. My mum will be helping me practise the routines.'

Despite briefly learning a Cha-cha-cha for her Children in Need appearance, Maisie says contemporary dance is her comfort zone at the moment.

'The dance I'm most looking forward to is probably Street/Commercial, because that's the only one that I think I'll be able to do,' she says. 'The Cha-cha-cha was challenging but a lot of fun, so I'm looking forward to doing that one as well.'

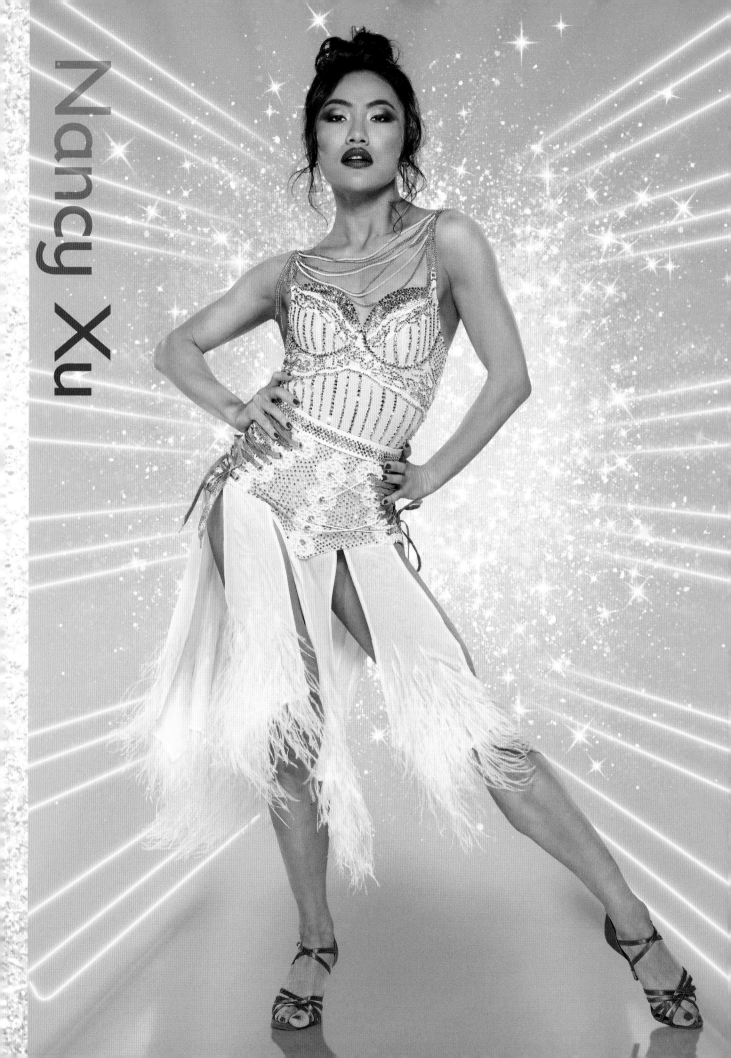

Nancy Xu

Returning for her second year on *Strictly Come Dancing*, Nancy Xu is bubbling with excitement.

'I really can't wait to start because I miss sharing the dance floor and going live with all the rest of the cast,' she says. 'The adrenaline, the dancing and all being together is something truly incredible!'

The Latin specialist says she settled in quickly last year and instantly felt part of the *Strictly* family.

'Last year was my first year on the show. Just imagine my feeling,' she says. 'It was a dream come true. My heart was full of love and happiness from the very beginning and all the cast were so friendly and welcoming to me. And, as always, the series was so good.'

Born in China, Nancy was a finalist in the U21 World Championships in 2010, took third place in the 2010–2012 CBDF National Amateur Latin Championships and was a runner-up at the 2013 Singapore International Dance Championship. She was also a finalist on *So You Think You Can Dance* in China. As a Latin queen, Nancy's favourite dances are the Paso Doble and the Rumba.

'I'm a lover of drama, and in the Paso and Rumba you can find, see and touch drama, story, romance and passion,' she says.

Ahead of the new series of *Strictly,* Nancy has been putting herself through some gruelling workouts as well as brushing up on her language skills.

'Since the last series I've studied a lot and tried to improve my English,' she says. 'I have also trained hard to keep myself fit. Before we started the official rehearsals, I was doing cardio training myself and dancing every day because, when I do something, I want to be able to give it 100 per cent.

'You can get fit doing lots of different things – cardio movements, running, body building, combat sports – but dance is different. I love dance because it melds with art and, at the end of the day, it is not just your body that gets fit, but also your mind and soul.

'Dance brings such a good feeling – in particular Latin dance, which brings sun and happiness to everyone,' she says. 'I hope *Strictly* is going to bring a beautiful mood to all the people who watch. It is one of the most followed TV shows in the country and the viewers love it so much. I always receive lots of messages from all the fans of the show saying that they can't wait to see us again because we bring them smiles, energy and positive vibes. I think they are so excited!'

ANSWERS

STRICTLY CROSSWORD

Aljaž Skorjanec
by *Janette Manrara*

Anton du Beke
by *Karen Hauer*

Graziano di Prima
by *Giovanni Pernice*

Dianne Buswell
by *Amy Dowden*

Janette Manrara
by *Aljaž Skorjanec*

Johannes Radebe
by *Oti Mabuse*

Nadiya Bychkova
by *Katya Jones*

Neil Jones
by *Graziano di Prima*

Oti Mabuse
by *Neil Jones*

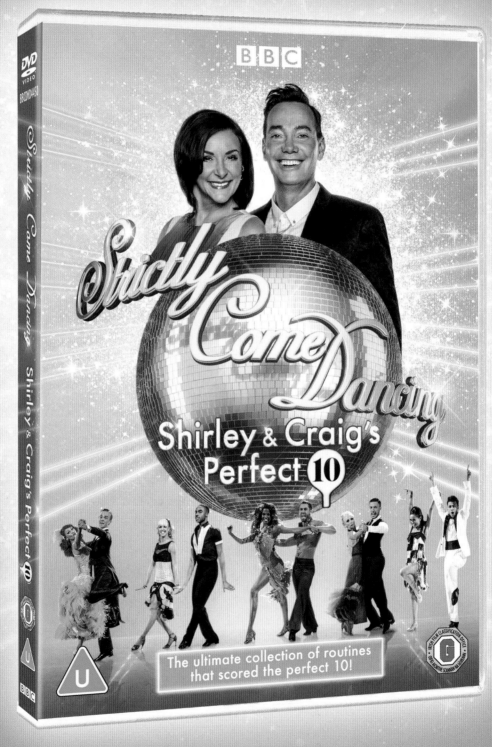